ON OUR WAY TO THE
SEVENTH DAY OF
CREATION

Donnia Treat Bradley

BALBOA.
PRESS

A DIVISION OF HAY HOUSE

Balboa Press books may be ordered through booksellers or by contacting:

Balboa Press
A Division of Hay House
1663 Liberty Drive
Bloomington, IN 47403
www.balboapress.com
1 (877) 407-4847

Print information available on the last page.

ISBN: 978-1-5043-9049-1 (sc)
ISBN: 978-1-5043-9051-4 (hc)
ISBN: 978-1-5043-9050-7 (e)

Library of Congress Control Number: 2017916635

Balboa Press rev. date: 11/01/2017

Contents

Preface

A S I LOOK BACK OVER my life, I cannot think of anyone I have crossed paths with who has not influenced this book. My siblings, parents, children, and relatives through birth or marriage have influenced my research and desire to write this book. I will be eternally grateful to all, in both living and no longer physical form, for their influence. Many of the people in my life will have a hard time accepting this, but I appreciate each of them for their input and opinions which have made it possible for me to put these words on paper especially my loving husband, Larry Bradley, who has supported me through all of my insanities since the day we met.

Without each of them I would never have begun to ask the big questions of what, why, when, and where. What is life all about? Why were we born? When will the suffering end? And last but far from least, where is this going to take us? I was eleven years old when I started asking why a church would teach anything other than the love of God and how someone could live life knowing of that love. Somehow I had an understanding within that love we were unlimited and I wanted to know why. I have spent my life trying to understand why we limit ourselves. If I were to have my way words like *can't, impossible, too hard, bored* and *tired* would all be removed from books. They are words with no meaning except to teach lessons we should have already learned. However, evolution takes time.

One of the many questions that boggles my mind is how can there be all these religions, teaching about all these rituals and yet not one focuses on the love of God? Why would God leave us so totally in the dark? What is the purpose of life at all? I had gone to many different churches with my grandmother, aunts, and siblings in my youth. What I saw was pain, suffering, loss, loneliness, and grief. What I heard from the teachers and preachers was guilt, fear, lack of understanding, untold mysteries, sadness, and more loneliness.

As a young adult I went to a black Baptist church. I had been to other Baptist churches but not like this one. Their music was upbeat and full of celebration of a loving God. I am not saying the preaching was not one of blame, sin, and guilt but their music was at least fun. When I returned to my own church it was the same sad and morose songs from last week. But which religion was right?

And I was just looking at varieties of Christianity. I had a few friends who were Buddhist and of course my church said that they were evil. But they were the nicest people I knew at the time. They were into nutrition and natural health and frankly they helped me more than doctors with all their natural remedies so I found myself asking why my church would say they were bad, and wasn't that judgment to condemn them? My church and its attitude made me start looking into Buddhism. That brought me the first revelation of my earlier life. I picked up a book at the library of Buddhist stories and the first chapter was a story of the flood. It had quite a few differences from "our" bible and so the search began. After reading every book on religion I could at our local library I had so many new thoughts, so many new questions.

I found myself buried in books and taking notes. But more importantly all the reading, searching and studying brought me to an experience that would change my life forever. I will save that story for later but that experience changed me to the point that some people close to me thought I was on drugs, but honestly, I was high on truth and life. I found myself receiving answers to all my questions, and life was suddenly exciting. I did not want to sleep, but when I did I would awaken excited, wondering what new would come into my life that day.

I found myself asking the hard questions such as; what were the prophecies about and what did the parables really mean? The answers would come either in words or by randomly picking up a book and having it fall open to the page with the answers. Sometimes it would be both. I would KNOW the answer and then when I went to the library a book or books would verify what I had come to KNOW. I lived in communication with something beyond myself that was wiser, more loving, and more aware. Something or someone was helping to make me live each day happier and more fulfilled until, I asked it to stop and go away.

If you ask for something enough you will receive it whether it is good or bad. When I went back to life as before, it was devastating and painful, but it was for what I felt was a greater purpose. So I struggled through life going through similar experiences that I had had before the voice and wisdom came. Then I went in and out of the process of growing and evolving multiple times until I GOT IT. I understood all the hard questions and knew I had a choice to make. That choice brought me here to writing this book to explain the Kingdom of Heaven and the purpose of life on this planet. I say these words are not mine because these are words that were 'downloaded' to me as I asked questions.

If you want to follow my journey you must read the book from front to back with no skipping around. If you skip around the book it will be like walking home from school. You might decide to take a turn here or there, out of curiosity, but you will no longer be on the path home. If you are not careful you could easily become lost.

This book has been a lifetime of questions and answers starting at age four when I first asked why I had to be "here." And why people do not listen and love each other. The answers arrived and I have tried to present my experiential lessons here within these pages. I hope you enjoy my journey.

Introduction

AFTER 18 MONTHS OF CONSTANT communication with what I refer to as "they" I was shocked to be told that humans have no idea how powerful humans are. This book is part of what I have learned over the last fifty years from "they." The reason "they" have no name is simply that information comes from many, not just a small group but a collective of teachers. I am taught by the expert in the field of inquiry. "They" only respond to my questions or needs at the time. The answers come from a myriad of teachers and sometimes I get what I refer to as a lie, but basically this is disinformation. This is why we have been told to discern the spirits. There are actually more spirits who do not have a clue, if you look around at the world this is evident. Which ones would you chose as your spiritual teachers and guides? It is the same in the ethereal world.

One very clear message I was given is it is difficult to convey wisdom from the more advanced realms of spirit simply because the same words we use in daily life have dual meanings. Words they use from the spiritual realm are common terms we use today but with these advanced beings the same words can mean something totally different. As an example I was told I needed to bring forth the Christ Child. Oh, my gosh! I already had four children that I was not too good with and now a Christ Child? I was freaked out to say the least. However, the meaning is we each have to birth the Christ that lives within us which is referred to as the Holy Spirit. This Spirit actually resides, like a small egg, in the area of the heart. As we open to total unconditional love and seek inside ourselves, this Christ awakens and teaches you from within. We have been taught by religions all our lives that

God is outside of us, but when God made us in His image He implanted the Holy Spirit within the human body. It is referred to as, "breathing life into the body." If the Spirit is not awakened you are as a dead person. It is just that simple. In fact, the entire process of evolving into an aware Spiritual Being in human form is simple, but you need to understand the process. This world is currently filled with more Spiritual teachers and guides than have ever been before on this planet in human form. My assignment as a teacher is to provide an understanding as to why they are here and why you would be drawn to accomplish this stage of your evolution.

In order to do this it is necessary to tell you the opposite of what I endeavor to come up with which is an understandable model. If you are a devout religionist the only way I can begin is to say **Absolutely everything man believes to be true about himself is a Total Misconception. All, but one fact, man believes to be true about God is a Total Misconception.** The only truth man believes about God, and he only half believes, is that God is Love. Karl Marx was absolutely right. Religion is nothing but the opiate of the people. It is man's survivalist nature that takes him into a fight or flight mode of being in this world. Because of this, man has been lead to believe he needs religion to make him feel guilty about absolutely everything he thinks, feels, and wants. Due to this, man has come to need religion to absolve him of his guilt. There are many people who will take exception to this. If it were not true, the correct religion would be so successful there would be no others. As a general rule, religions do not lead people astray out of desire. They do it out of ignorance and continued misinformation. That misinformation is promulgated by governmental leaders who, out of greed and the maniacal desire for power, encourage the misinformation and ignorance. It is their desire to keep humankind in ignorance; this was the goal behind the removal of Jesus as a teacher. Had Jesus succeeded in His teachings man would have taken that next step of evolving and the need for governing bodies would have shifted into something that empowers and provides.

Religion; its rules and regulations, are a means to control man and nothing more. The priests, rulers, and leaders know the only way they can control man is to prevent him from knowing exactly what mankind is truly capable of. Once man evolves into his full abilities, powers, and knowledge no group can control or subdue him and there will no longer be a need for controlling humanity.

If Buddhism worked there would be no Calcutta, poverty, or starvation, nor would the Dalai Lama have been forced to leave Lhasa Tibet. Who would choose starvation and poverty as a preferred way of life? If Judaism worked, there would not have been the exodus or Hitler. If the Native American religions and spiritual practices were as perfect as so many now try to make them, there would not have been a General Custer or the slaughter of so many Native Americans. The failings of Christianity are just as disastrous and vast. Ashach, Meshah, and Abendigo could stand unburned in a fiery furnace, but at the same time, as reported through biblical stories, God turned his back on all the Christians who were killed by gladiators or thrown to the lions. It is a misconception that man must suffer to be wise. It is true that man chooses to suffer rather than seek his own inner nature and truth.

Can anyone accept that the select minority of Islam is following a righteous teaching when it breeds so much violence? Of course not. But are we any more correct by saying that we must be more accepting of THEIR TRUTH OR THEIR WAYS? N0! Religion is the opiate of the people. If religions were correct we would have to assume that God is quite selective when he saves only three from the fire and the rest are not important. Unfortunately, tragedy exists for two reasons. One, it is a tool available to stimulate people to realize what they are. Two, it is the result of ignorance of who and what man is and who and what God is. It is as simple as that. If man understood these two truths, there would be no need for pain or suffering. Man would not allow suffering to happen even to the mass murderer, who only exists because of ignorance. The same is true of any sexual predator, murderer, or any other kind of criminal. As each man becomes aware of who and what he is, then ALL pain and suffering diminishes.

The greatest of truth bringers such as prophets and Christ tried to convey this message, but once you achieve the state of knowing who and what you are, it is almost totally impossible to communicate to the masses at their level of his understanding. There is no language to explain God to man when you are at the transitory state that occurs once you are awakened to the level of comprehension of who and what you are as a physical/spiritual being. Each religion likes to believe that its path has only failed because "not everyone practices properly" or too many people "sin." Each religion also has its own concept of sin or improper practice of rituals.

Everything about the structure man has devised upon the face of the earth is only driving him further from who and what he really is. It is a fact that this statement takes me out of the realm of "true compassion and understanding." How compassionate and understanding could I be if I chose to sugar coat truth and lie to you? Many men have tried to explain this, Buddha, Christ, Mohammad, Pythagoras, Nisargadatta, and Kahlil Gibran to name a few. They have tried to explain what man is in a loving way that would draw men toward the truth. But, like much of the New Age movement, it sugar coats the fact that everything man believes to be true about the self and God is, in fact, a fabrication of inaccurate facts.

Our educational system is the worst system we have in place. We do not need to program our children to remember facts and perform tasks. All we need is to remind children that they are eternal beings with all their memories intact and that teaching should start long before a desired conception not when the children become adults. Children need to be taught to understand their responsibilities relating to their own past lives in order to ascertain how to make decisions in this life. When these two systems are established, then all other systems will be working, functional models from education to our financial and governmental structures.

Everyone loves to hate the government, but it is actually the most functional system we have at this time. It is neither compassionate nor honest, but it does function to the full capacity it was designed to function within. It takes the things we choose not to deal with and provides the funds for government to do it. This even includes keeping the poor from the not so poor allowing us to feel no guilt or shame associated with their plight. When you farm out someone else to shoot your dog, don't complain about how they shoot him. We farm out to our government what we feel are burdensome, distasteful tasks; so don't complain about how the government does it. We will not do these jobs ourselves or we would have no need for government to begin with. All we really want from our government is to keep the poor off the streets, keep the country running in general, and to go to war with those who are threats and keep those who disagree out of our daily lives. It is a just and efficient system for what it is designed to do.

Do you realize how many distasteful tasks we have delegated to governmental agencies to manage for us? We have given government responsibility over the education of our children and adults. The decision of who to agree with and disagree with is in our government's hands. By citizens giving them this power the government can then decide who we must dispense with and we call this process war. The government has taken over what once was the responsibility of neighbors and churches because we have set up the Department of Human Services better known as Health and Welfare.

We don't even want to be responsible for what we put into our bodies so we have the Food and Drug administration. God forbid we make a morphine addict out of a man who is suffering from the final days of cancer. How unconscionable would that be? We require the government to make these distasteful decisions for us. Then there is the need for government to regulate agriculture, import/export, our financial structure, freedom of religion, and so many more aspects of life that man does not want to deal with on a daily basis. It appears making decisions or discerning what is good or bad, right or wrong, has become too burdensome to us. We choose to give that control and decision making power to our government and then we devote multiple hours complaining about the control government has over our lives. A simple example of this is daylight savings time. Everyone hates daylight savings time yet we do nothing to change it except for a few individual states. We allow our government to dictate to us rules and laws that no longer serve us.

However, you cannot have it both ways. You either pay the government taxes to do all the tasks too burdensome or distasteful to you or you do it yourself. As society stands today, I do not believe man has the capacity to operate without government structure and control.

Enough about our government. All we need know is what Christ meant when he said:

> **Matt. 22:21 ASV** *'Render therefore unto **Caesar** the things that are **Caesar's**; and unto God what is God's'.*

In other words, do not waste your time fighting the government. Accept the government for what it was designed to do and pay your taxes to do it. Use your time finding out who and what man really is. If you want to stop the government, become who and what you are and then the government will fall away due to lack of need. This is exactly what I was saying about control. The government never wanted man to know who and what he is which is exactly why Christ was crucified to begin with. Once you reach this state of realization you have absolutely no need of governmental control and regulation. Now you can understand why the government wanted to stop Him.

Christ said quite plainly:

> **John 10:34 ASV** *"Have I not said 'You are Gods,' Jesus answered them, 'Is it not written in your law, I said, Ye are gods?'*

You are not the one and only God but a part of the totality of God. You are a part of the whole. All is God. Therefore, you are God. The tree is God. The grass is God. The air is God, etc., etc. Everything being subjective then EVERYTHING is God means <u>everything</u> not just what you choose to accept as God. Hitler was part of God. Osama Bin Laden was part of God as is Billy Graham, Deepak Chopra, all the United States Presidents, and all other political and spiritual leaders as well as terrorists and criminals.

We will establish a process that will bring you into a closer realization of who and what you are. Then we will have the ability to develop a greater understanding regarding the purpose of government and religion on the furtherance of man and society as a whole. In other words we will begin to establish the beginnings of subjective truth to bring the world into what Christ referred to as the Kingdom of God. When asked where is Heaven? Christ replied:

> **Luke 17:21 ASV** *'Therefore lo, the kingdom of God is within you.'*

Chapter One

THE SIXTH DAY-
DEMYSTIFYING CREATION

Have you ever wondered how Moses received information to write the Books of the Pentateuch? Can you imagine that source explaining the details of creating the Heavens and Earth, and how man six thousand years ago could possibly comprehend a big bang process? Take into consideration that Moses would not even have the simple sciences you learned in grade school. Imagine explaining the molecular process of the beginnings of life on planet earth. He might have heard something like, 'so Moses, first of all there was this big bang and everything exploded,' and God started evolution. Or should we just say, in the beginning God created the Heavens and the Earth?

Along those same lines, few have a real understanding of the Darwinian Theory of Evolution. On one hand, the most obvious detail is that humans have evolved from apes. On the other hand, many choose to reject evolution based upon that one objection. Is it possible both are right? Can we put the two side by side and take that into consideration, since we do not have total molecular details, that both are credible?

In the early 1970s I was presented with an opportunity to be the teacher in my Sunday school class. Our teacher needed six weeks off and asked if class members would volunteer to fill in for him. I decided this would be a great opportunity to test the information I had been receiving about evolution. After some consideration, I took a deep breath and said an even deeper prayer then volunteered for one Sunday.

I will simplify my lesson by providing a simple comparative chart showing the order of creation relative to Darwin's theory.

Bible	Darwin
Creation of heaven and earth	Big Bang forming heaven and earth
Separation land from water	Separation land from water
Appearance of light and dark	Appearance of light and dark
Water swarms with living things	Water swarms with living things
Creation of birds and flying creatures	Creation of birds and flying creatures
Creation of larger sea creatures	Creation of larger sea creatures
Creation of creatures on the land	Creation of creatures on the land
And now man	And now man

By the time I reached this part of the talk, thirteen out of fourteen students were very impressed and considering the fact that there was no difference. I had not reached the punch line yet though and I was anxious to hear their response.

These are the first two points most people are unaware of. God made man in his image and gave him dominion over everything in the sea, air, and on land. That means man is now responsible to manage and take care of these living creatures. And again something interesting is brought to the surface. God blessed everything and said, be fruitful, and multiply, and then He said something no one ever spoke of. He said replenish the earth and subdue it. Now, replenish means it must be populated <u>again</u> which would imply the existence of life <u>before</u> animals and man were created.

But there are more revelations when we look at:

> **Genesis 2:2 ASV** *'And on the seventh day God finished his work which he had made; and he rested on the seventh day from all his work which he had made.'*

The ramifications of this statement are huge. This implies we are now in the image of God. I accept that God is total perfection and at the same time a conscious creator, so let's break this down as it was explained to me. Point one; man is not perfect. Point two; we are not conscious creators. Point three; we are in-between the sixth and seventh ice age, which means we have not entered the seventh period of existence. I am convinced, because of these three points we have not yet reached the seventh day. We have not yet reached perfection or completion in the creation process. And Darwin is no longer significant in this process because his only points of reference were in the physical evolution which did imply the Bibles path of creation.

Now we come to point four. When you were created you came from human parents who made you a physical being born of water. When born of God, you recognize yourself as a spiritual being and this knowing will bring about perfection. Many people understand this intellectually and believe they have experienced this. In truth, only a few have and those who achieved oneness with the Spiritual have no words to explain what it is or how to attain it. In fact few of the "Living-Ones" can relate how they achieved that level of awareness or awakening. They arrived but have no idea of the process so it is impossible to share with others.

Their only knowledge is they were changed instantly or over a period of time.

Once achieving this level of awareness you will no longer be tempted to break the Ten Commandments or commit what is mistakenly referred to as sin. For you, those traits or desires will not exist because you will have evolved and matured into a Son of God. You will now be a brother of Jesus and a Christ, as Jesus is. We are not there yet.

I realize this sounds very foreign to most readers. We are taught by religions to do this ritual and that, and keep trying to be better. But those times are drawing to an end. One day we will understand that Freedom of Choice is the greatest gift God gave us. But I want to refer back to:

> ***Genesis 2:1-4 ASV*** *'And the heavens and the earth were finished, and all the host of them. And on the seventh day God finished his work which he had made; and he rested on the seventh day from all his work which he had made. And God blessed the seventh day, and hallowed it; because that in it he rested from all his work which God had created and made. These are the generations of the heavens and of the earth when they were created, in the day that Jehovah God made earth and heaven.'*

This says that it is finished; the process of creation is complete. Man has evolved to perfection and God rested, but as I said we are not there yet. We are still in the sixth day. However:

> ***Genesis 2:5 ASV*** *'And no plant of the field was yet in the earth, and no herb of the field had yet sprung up; for Jehovah God had not caused it to rain upon the earth: and there was not a man to till the ground.'*

One verse says it is finished and the next verse says the seeds and plants were not there and neither was man. But the previous verses say God had created man. The reason for this is very easy to understand. Genesis 1:1 ASV through Genesis 2:4 ASV is a synopsis of the creation of earth and heaven from beginning to completion. Genesis 2:5 ASV is the beginning of a new chapter or book which should say, these are the details of how the creation of earth and the heavens were accomplished. Now we will continue to the details of life during the sixth day of creation.

This is the first example of verses being overlooked or not understood. Many are confused with:

> **Matt. 24:34 ASV** *'Verily I say unto you, This generation shall not pass away, till all these things be accomplished.'*

What is being referred to as 'accomplished' is the coming of the Son of God upon the clouds. Note the reference to "this generation". The generation when Jesus passed from earth over two thousand years ago is within the time of the sixth day. The reference is to this generation, one between the ice ages and of man in his sixth day of creation. We shall see the Son of God return before the next ice age and the arrival of the seventh day. That is the only time frame Jesus could have been referring to because a generation of man at the time of Jesus could be from thirty-two to seventy years but would certainly not last over two thousand years. So 'generation' had to refer to the same level of evolution or the sixth day of creation and we have not entered into the seventh day.

For a deeper understanding as to what this generation of man consists of we must return to the discussion of creation. It is stated that man is made in the image of God. You are born of physical parents which makes you a physical being. But when you were made into the image of God you became a Spiritually Being, not a Charlton Heston look-alike from the movies. That image is a vengeful, judgmental and angry God floating somewhere in the clouds and is not true. God is unconditional love and has given man the freedom of choice. I am here to tell you that God gives you absolutely nothing you do not ask for, absolutely nothing.

Even in man's own ignorance of who and what he is, man is in total control of his own life and destiny. It is man's choice to be exactly what he is, whether he is murderer or saint. In this generation, man is evolving into a being that understands his universe and role in it. He has gone from learning how to make tools, wheels, and rudimentary survival needs into beings that can go to the moon, circle the stars, take DNA and separate it out into perfection so the body will be disease free and live forever as it was created to do. This generation of man has always controlled DNA even though it was out of ignorance and accomplished through an involuntary act of Karma which is only a short name for 'what you reap so will you sow.' Unfortunately, all too often man creates from fear and survival needs, not out of the desire for a life he chooses but even from that unaware state man is in control of his own DNA.

This generation of man remains ignorant to the fact that he could be a God even though he was created in the image of God. Just as in physical form you are not your biological father but can be more because your father tries to impart his life lessons and wisdom to you. You are capable of becoming more than your physical father. Just as with God, you are created in His image. You cannot be God, but you can be like God for the same reasons. God has imparted His wisdom and capabilities to you; therefore, you have the ability to be a God, but not THE God of creation.

Man has learned survival skills, established schools, and communication systems both verbal and digital. He has invented methods of travel that would have shocked the minds of lesser thinking men hundreds of years ago, but even then there were visionaries who saw 'vehicles' that transported man from one location to another. This generation has learned to control his environment through heating and air conditioning. They have built highways, airports, and grocery stores eliminating the need to grow one's own food or trading for it. They have even explored the moon and mars. Man has evolved.

However, this generation of man is not unlike those who lived ten thousand years ago. The current generation or type of human is referred to as 'Anatomically Modern Humans.' Many say Anatomically Modern Humans appeared independent of evolution over two hundred thousand years ago with the same DNA we have today, but were unaware they were Spiritual Beings. God had not breathed 'His life,' what is referred to as the Holy Spirit, into all mankind at that time. However, man is the same, he learns, builds, creates, and imagines. He thinks of himself as a human being subject to something greater than he perceives himself to be. This generation of man advances technologically but refuses to look in the mirror and ask, "Who and what am I?" This generation has become convinced, mostly through religious teachings that we must suffer through illness, war, accidents, pain, and deprivation at the hands of their own governmental structure and that of other nations. Plus we are constantly reminded, within religious circles, that 'God will not give us more suffering than we can bear'. That statement puts me on edge. Why would a God who loves you unconditionally give you any suffering?

The most accurate way to describe this generation of man is as a linear thinking, three dimensional creature. Even though man has always looked for something outside of himself to be responsible for his actions and way of being in the world, he classifies himself as being responsible for his actions with a right to choose how he thinks and lives in the world. Meanwhile, he personifies himself as a victim of circumstances unaware that each particle or mass that exists has intelligence, is controlled, and is formed into existence by whatever man reasons to be true.

And exactly how is this manifested into being within our daily lives? Christ spoke often in parables, stories relating to the way man was living during Christ's time in physical form. These parables were never meant to be a mystery but examples of how life would be in the Kingdom of Heaven using instances from two thousand years ago in the area of the world which is now Israel, Iraq, and Iran. Many are unaware that Bethlehem was not far from what is now Baghdad. So parables were of fig trees, vineyards, and oil lamps. These tales were familiar to the people of that time.

Today, if you were comparing the vastness of God to the limitations of humankind a parable might be comparing a gnat to man. A gnat has a short and limited life span. It remains in a relatively small portion of the world often just within a house or a block area. The gnats purpose is eat, reproduce, and survive. It is unaware that man exists or the scope of his existence other than as an element in the gnats world. He has no concept of what man is nor does he stop and question what man is. A gnat simply lives and dies just being a gnat. In comparison, the majority of humanity is unaware of the scope, abilities and functions of God. Man just lives and dies ignoring God OR hoping he will arrive in heaven. Man lives a limited life which is a very tiny portion of what is within God's world. This cannot simply be referred to as the universe or our solar system because we only see those as three dimensional at this level/generation of evolving. God's world is not limited by dimensions, space or time and as those aspects are what man relates to it is difficult to explain or classify God. We are aware there is 'something' greater than ourselves and that this 'something' has power and energy of unexplainable form, yet somehow, through teachings of religion and movies, man has lowered God to be in the image of man. Eventually we will understand that He is the cause and effect within our lives. At that time we will have moved past this generation of man.

If God is:

Matt. 6:9 ASV *"Our Father who art in Heaven"*

... Then we have two points of knowable reference we can relate to:

A) God is a parental figure and based upon experience within our own family structure. We use this model to classify God. In other words, if God as your parent was judgmental, angry, unsatisfied in life, and incapable of nurturing other than providing the food you ate and clothes you wore, then you would classify God as one interested only in your survivalist needs. However, if you were more fortunate and had a parent who taught and encouraged you so that you could achieve your dreams and goals then your vision of God as one who provides what you want. Still, he is a parent and limited within the linear, dimensional views experienced at this generational, evolutionary state of being.

B) We know where God is. God is in Heaven. We are told Heaven is "up there", and when we die, that is where we will go. This presents us with another important fact about God. He is inaccessible and in a place we cannot reach except through direct prayer to Jesus as an intermediary to God; or unless we die.

Just as the gnat's viewpoint of man is limited by its own personal experience so is our experience of God limited. And even these terms are linear, three dimensional limitations and have absolutely nothing to do with who or what God is. Every particle of mass or energy has some intelligence within it as we have come to understand with the help of quantum physics. All mass and energy is in a transitional phase on its own evolutionary path. We will understand these quantum particles more as we move on to an understanding of how we create our own lives and our own understanding of reality.

This is a tiny attempt to explain the state of life that exists in this current generation of man. Man believes he is the victim of uncontrollable circumstances outside of himself. He also believes he can only think positive and TRY to do what is best. Man believes God will not "give him more than he can bear." As these concepts fall away and man becomes aware of other dimensions and realities, this generation shall become a new generation of a new type of man living in the seventh day of creation.

Many messages can become clear when the true meaning of 'this generation' is realized and we accept that we have not passed into the seventh day of creation. It is called the Pleistocene Epoch and more specifically the Holocene ice age. I am not a Paleontologist but there have been six Epochs. Right now we are in the middle or later part of the sixth. The previous five were the <u>Huronian</u>, <u>Cryogenian</u>, <u>Andean-Saharan</u>, <u>Karoo Ice Age,</u> and the <u>Quaternary glaciation</u>. Each of these stages coincides with the Biblical Story of Creation of the first five days. Science and the Bible have never been in conflict. In fact, they have each exemplified the other. We have all wondered at the idea that to God one day is as a thousand years, and a thousand years as one day. So here it is, in black and white. Six days also equals the six epochs, ices ages, time periods, etc., each time period consisting of millions of years. That is, the sixth day of man, the sixth age of life on planet earth. In fact, it explains the number of the beast perfectly, the anti-Christ.

As a Christian, one of the first things you learn is that God is three-fold consisting of the Father, the Son, and the Holy Ghost. Having been made in the image of God man is also three-fold. Man is a body, mind, and spirit. Therefore, if the body is in the sixth day, the mind is the sixth day and the spirit is in the sixth day, man is the six-six-six or the anti-Christ. If man remains stuck at the sixth day of creation level before the return of Christ then man is unaware of the Christ or anti-Christ. By refusing to accept that the Spirit of Christ is to be born within us then we are against the Christ. There is only one sin unto death and it is blasphemy. I spent many years researching and verifying that, in fact, blasphemy means you are against the Spirit that is to be born within. So the Spirit is within you at birth but you must awaken it within you. So of course, you would be classified as dead. This information must settle in and be digested in order to truly understand this reference. At first it seems impossible and unacceptable. But this is not about all of man being the anti-Christ; it is about a possible few stuck in this level of evolution and unable to move onto the seventh day of creation. In itself, it is a notice of possibilities, something we should all become aware of the possibility we could miss or at the very least delay our own evolution by accepting this generation, the sixth day of evolution, is all there is.

How easy would it be for that to happen? Again our belief is based on two kinds of truth and unless it is experiential it is not real to the individual. If one finds themselves entrenched within the structure of Christianity or any religion, it would be quite easy to continue accepting the religious dogma as truth because the way of man seems natural but the path to the Kingdom of Heaven is narrow and steep. In other words, staying stuck at the sixth level of evolution, within the sixth day is easy and natural. This is why I am sharing the benefits of the wisdom to be open-minded and look inside to find the path to your full evolution into the Son of God.

It is also important we understand the message from the past, 'if your eye is single pluck it out as a reference to being narrow or single minded.' You see with one eye, one way. The eye of course represents what you see and therefore influences what you believe. It refers to being single-minded, narrow-minded, closed-minded or living with tunnel vision because one eye only sees the world one way. A closed mind cannot understand the Bible or the Word of God. Do not let others deceive you. Do not let others, not even me; tell you what the Bible truly means. Read it for yourself with an open mind. That's not an easy task since most of us have years of teachers, preachers, news media, television shows, and social media telling us what to think and what the Bible and God means.

In reading the Bible for yourself, ask this same question I

originally asked. How did Moses receive the information to write the Books of the Pentateuch? Many believe God spoke to him. It is a common practice today for people to receive channeled information. Often they receive the names of the entities from where they received the information. However, I have yet to hear anyone stating they spoke with God directly. I have been receiving information from an informed source for over 49 years now and I do believe, that one morning, I received a communication directly from God letting me know that God is total unconditional love. Then, I 'thought' I was receiving information from Jesus, but I am no longer convinced that was the source. After much thought, consideration, and prayer this verse came to my attention.

> **I Corinthians 12:10 ASV** *'and to another workings of miracles; and to another prophecy; and to another discerning of spirits: to another divers kinds of tongues; and to another the interpretation of tongues.'*

I had been taught at church that this verse was about deciding who was a good or bad person. But it does not say 'discern people.' It says 'discern spirits.' I began to be more aware of the information I was receiving and realized some of it was deceptive, but most of it was in direct response to what I was asking.

The point is, while you are reading the Bible and asking questions, discern the Spirit of the answers you receive and who is providing those answers. Keep your mind open and pliable but not so open that even wrong answers stay in your mind. Ask yourself often, would God who is TOTAL love do something like that and is this answer in line with what I know to be true about God, Jesus, and the creation of the heavens and the earth? And ask my favorite question, 'what would Jesus do?'

Also ponder who talked to Moses. Who actually spoke the words of the beginning and completion of the heavens and the earth to Moses? Where do all of these channelers receive their information? As I said, many of them provide names but if queried, admit the names are actually of a group of people and not just one or two individuals. This leads to the concept of the Collective Unconscious, a theory that has been around for many years. However, the original concept was based on the idea that evil and negative emotions are powerful and can become a form of universal energy and emotions that exists all around us. If you are open and susceptible you can be "overcome" by this universal negative energy. It has been hypothesized that this is one of the reasons seemingly well-balanced individuals can suddenly become out-of-control monsters and inflict harm upon others.

All thoughts have energy and become a living thought form which remains active until dealt with. This means if you hate your mother or even a stranger, that hate becomes a living energy and must manifest itself in some way before it dissipates. This Universal Unconscious can come from Higher Beings who have been Masters forever, or from beings that learned in human form how to raise their knowingness, and even from less knowledgeable beings. This is why we must discern the Spirits that present information to us.

I went through quite a process to determine which information was valid and which was 'vain imaginings.' When we first start receiving information it can come from all levels of knowing and emotions, but as we sort the real truths from erroneous facts, we begin to realize a greater level of understanding. Once this wiser level of receiving is achieved we establish that as our own vibration and level of learning. In time, we are able to maintain this communication while being in the world but not of it. Now we see the truth of life around us without judgment.

This is no different than it is on the physical plane. We move according to our frequencies and electro-magnetic fields. By that I mean people are either drawn to you, repelled by you or are indifferent. We are drawn together by commonality of interests, goals, and desires. We move in circles filled with people who share common interests. If you have children then you will most likely be involved with other parents or children of a similar age group. If you are interested in service such as the Red Cross or feeding the hungry then you will be around people who are interested in the same thing. If you are a drug addict, alcoholic, or criminal chances are you will communicate on a daily basis with others who share that interest.

The same is true in the Spiritual realm. Spiritual Beings are drawn to you by your abilities and interests. However, on the earth plane our paths are frequently crossed with people we have nothing in common with as well as those with extreme differences in energies and interests than ours. That is why we have accidents or cross paths with extremely negative or positive people. It is up to the individual to discern and decide if they want to engage in more serious contact with the spirits. Many make the mistake of engaging them and learn that you should not listen to the more negative of Spirits.

The point is that thoughts have a life of their own. They generate energy and information that is constantly being downloaded whether we are aware of it or not. You can see this when working on an invention or researching information on the internet. Perhaps you have had a particular idea that might be helpful for you or people you care about, when researching on a computer you find many people are asking the same question or researching the same fact. Or, other people working on the same idea you had. It has been said, 'there is no new thought under the sun,' and once you're open to this concept you will see that this is fact.

Chapter Two

KNOW THE TRUTH

W HAT DRIVES OR MOTIVATES THE individual to seek out the God of their childhood? The reason we need to consider this question is because different methods work for those with different motivations. There is also a differentiation based on the personality and health of the seeker. That may sound strange but hopefully it will become clearer as we discuss this. Another factor is whether they are open-minded or blind followers of a particular religion or sect outside of Christianity.

Like many seekers I have spoken with over the years, my childhood was filled with depression and confusion. I'd always felt as though a contract had been broken. I felt I was to have a specific kind of life and found the life I was living was not <u>this</u> life. I did not want to be in this body or in this life at all and my health has always paid the price for those feelings.

By age twenty-one, I was the mother of four babies. At twenty-three, with an abusive alcoholic husband, I had filed for divorce. For the sake of the children and my own sanity I had to leave. But I was conflicted.

I felt as though I could not live without him, but I knew my four children were faced with a very bleak future if I did not leave him. I was depressed and on so many medications, I was on the verge of becoming a drug addict.

As a child, even though my parents did not take us to church my siblings and I attended most Sunday mornings without fail. I loved church. I learned so much while feeling love and hope from the teachings of Jesus. So now, in the middle of another unbearable hardship, I found myself seeking that same comfort.

Time passed and I became involved with a man who was deployed to Vietnam, supposedly given one of the safest jobs there. Ninety days before he was to return home he was killed. Now, at twenty-five, I felt as though I was losing my mind. I had dropped out of school by the end of my sophomore year and I had no job skills or education. By the grace of God Cessna hired me to help build engine firewalls for two of their trainer jets. The job at Cessna was a great gift for more reasons than the obvious.

My job was what would be called a Rosie the Riveter job. I had a partner and together we would assemble engine firewalls. My partner was a woman my age, recently divorced, who was very religious and went to church all the time. We often talked about faith and hope. However, drilling and riveting is very loud and noisy so all chit chat was saved for breaks and lunch.

I spent most of the noisy part of the day talking to myself, or so I thought. I asked questions like, "God if you love me so much why do you want me to suffer?" And I would also ask about the Bible verses. In fact, I had Bible verses going through my head all day long. Sometimes it would be the same one over and over again until I understood it. I mostly learned how parables were used to help people understand what Jesus was saying. So, when I considered that the stories consisted of elements from his time; like oil lamps, servants, and fig trees, then replaced them with elements common to me, like electric lights, employees, and apple trees the 'parables' became clear to me.

I am going to share what this process consisted of on a daily basis. Keep in mind, my life was in chaos and I was desperate for answers. I was obsessed.

This is how information came to me. First a verse would come into my head:

John 8:32 ASV *'And ye shall know the truth, and the truth shall make you free.'*

Then I would immediately receive an explanation like this: With one exception about truth which is, "truth is totally relative to the person, time and situation that they are currently experiencing." Nothing else is truth to those who experience it except the truth you experience and know for yourself. Another person's truth can have nothing to do with you unless you yourself have come to know and experience that truth for yourself.

There are two different kinds of truth. The first is the truth you know from fact. You may accept the truth through the reputation or trust of another and their teachings. This kind of truth exists as common knowledge. The second is the truth you know to be true because of personal experience. This is experiential truth. This is the only real truth to an individual. If you have no experience to know a fact is true then all it can be is an abstract fact with an assumed basis. In other words, until you experience a truth for yourself it is only abstract fact.

Truth changes for each generation. What is true for your parents or your children is not necessarily true for you. As man evolves and becomes more civilized and aware of what is right or wrong, acceptable or not acceptable, then the concept of truth changes. Also, what is true for your kindred, your ethnicity, or your group is rarely true to another's kindred, ethnicity or group. Truth is relevant to the experiencer in his own time and space. This is why there are so many assumed prophets and teachers. Prophets and teachers only prophesized or taught relevant to their time or space both physically and spiritually. The only exception to this rule of relevancy was Christ. As Jesus, he taught in relevance to his time, but who He was as the Christ was totally different. We will examine the uniqueness of Christ and what that brought to men for many generations. Other prophets taught relative truth but Christ taught a truth that can and will become totally experiential.

The statement, 'Know the truth and the truth shall make you free,' is only true if it is the second kind of truth. For example, you have been told all your life that fire burns, typically you accept that as the 'first truth'; information from someone you trust. Once you physically experience being burned yourself, it is the 'second truth'. In understanding that truth shall set you free be aware if it is totally your truth and not the truth others have inflicted upon you.

Some therapists have the ability to know what your lessons are in this lifetime and why you came into this body. Many people have that ability today. But that is the 'first truth', a factual truth. Yes, we can see where you are coming from. Yes, we can see where this is true. Until you have the 'second truth,' the Experiential Truth, it does not set you free. Factual truth only imprisons you. If all you have are the facts without proof of experience, you continue to question the facts.

To understand the two kinds of truth, let's start by looking at the life of Jesus and what the Bible tells us. Movies and plays have portrayed Jesus as a mild man with quiet mannerisms, however, that is not what I read. The Bible tells of a strong, independent thinking, outspoken person. He starts out having the nerve to walk straight into the temple and to the priests.

> *Luke 2:46-47 ASV* '⁴⁶ *And it came to pass, after three days they found him in the temple, sitting in the midst of the teachers, both hearing them, and asking them questions:* ⁴⁷ *and all that heard him were amazed at his understanding and his answers.'*

Not only did He talk to the priests, He also stayed for three days learning and teaching. That does not sound like a quiet, mild-mannered person. It sounds like a free-thinker, one who is self-assured and outspoken.

We tend to establish many lifelong opinions in our youth. I can remember my Sunday school teacher talking about Jesus as though He were a quiet, well-mannered young man who always stayed out of the way and agreed with everyone. Like others, I watched movies, listened to my teachers and thought of Jesus as a meek but determined person. After becoming a devout Bible student and reading on my own, the story of twelve year old Jesus teaching priests in the temple does not portray that image. Absolutely nothing about Jesus in the Bible resembled the one in the movies, stories, or my teacher's versions.

Next was His encounter with John the Baptist. John was very well thought of, popular, and important. People always surrounded John; yet Jesus walked right up to him and said, "Baptize me." John did not want to do that because he knew who He was and felt Jesus should baptize him. Determined, Jesus insisted John baptize Him. This is not a shy retiring man.

These two stories are not that different from our vision of Jesus, however others paint a very vivid opposite picture.

> **Luke 7:34 ASV** *'The Son of man is come eating and drinking; and ye say, Behold a gluttonous man, and a winebibber, a friend of publicans and sinners!'*

Here, He is referred to as gluttonous, a winebibber, and a friend; mind you, of publicans and sinners. He was actually reported as one who preferred bars and prostitutes to priests and teachers.

In fact, He was quite outspoken about His feelings. Six times in Matthew, Jesus speaks saying:

> **Matt. 23:13 ASV** *'Woe unto you, scribes and Pharisees, hypocrites!'*

What is a scribe? They were considered to be one of a learned class in ancient Israel through New Testament times studying the Scriptures who served as copyists, editors, teachers, and jurists. They were also classified as an official, or public secretary, or clerk, or a copier of manuscripts. And a Pharisee was a member of a Jewish sect noted for strict observance of rites and ceremonies of the written law, and for insistence on the validity of their own oral traditions concerning the law. So these two groups were considered wise in the teachings of that current religion. This same story is recounted in Luke eleven. These were not average, uneducated persons of the city.

Does Jesus sound meek making these statements? He is portrayed as someone not only confident, but also determined and outspoken. He challenged men of the religious law, not only telling them they didn't know what they were talking about, they didn't follow their own teachings as well. He was quite emphatic with His 'Woe to you Scribes and Pharisees. You are hypocrites.' He was aggressive, strong, and today He would be referred to as a know-it-all or a heretic. So, what exactly is a heretic?

A) A dissenter from established church dogma; especially: a baptized member of the Roman Catholic Church who disavows a revealed truth.

B) One who dissents from an accepted belief or doctrine.

He also is a dissenter. The story of His anger at those who sold their wares in the temple is a well-known story.

> ***Matt. 21:13 ASV*** *'And Jesus went into the temple of God, and cast out all them that sold and bought in the temple, and overthrew the tables of the moneychangers, and the seats of them that sold doves, And said unto them, It is written, My house shall be called the house of prayer; but ye have made it a den of thieves.'*

Mark 11:15-17 ASV '*And they come to Jerusalem: and he entered into the temple, and began to cast out them that sold and them that bought in the temple, and overthrew the tables of the money-changers, and the seats of them that sold the doves;* [16] *and he would not suffer that any man should carry a vessel through the temple.* [17] *And he taught, and said unto them, Is it not written, My house shall be called a house of prayer for all the nations? but ye have made it a den of robbers.*'

John 2:14-16 ASV '*And he found in the temple those that sold oxen and sheep and doves, and the changers of money sitting:* [15] *and he made a scourge of cords, and cast all out of the temple, both the sheep and the oxen; and he poured out the changers' money, and overthrew their tables;* [16] *and to them that sold the doves he said, Take these things hence; make not my Father's house a house of merchandise.*'

And when Jesus went to His friend Lazarus, He did not go quietly. He was upset. Someone He knew quite well who He had been teaching and showing the Way and Truth had died. Jesus was upset because He had taught Lazarus that he was more, but Lazarus did not believe. Now Jesus had to save Lazarus from himself. He did not speak quietly and meekly.

John 11:43-44 ASV '*And when he had thus spoken, he cried with a loud voice, Lazarus, come forth.* [44] *He that was dead came forth, bound hand and foot with* ¹*grave-clothes; and his face was bound about with a napkin. Jesus saith unto them, Loose him, and let him go.*'

Nothing about <u>this</u> Jesus was anything except commanding and exhibiting His God Given rights, even over death. Jesus was not quiet, serene, and charismatic. He is portrayed that way in movies and plays yet the Bible paints an entirely different picture. He didn't even convince His own disciples He was all He claimed to be. Even though they stood by Him, they still doubted and questioned everything about Him.

When He was arrested and it came time for the common people to choose between Jesus and a thief name Barabbas, very few spoke up for Jesus. I will not recount this story but it can be found *in Matt. 27 ASV, Mark 15 ASV, Luke 23 ASV* and *John 18 ASV.* He did not walk softly and carry a big stick. Jesus knew exactly who and what He was. He was the first-born Son of God. He did not apologize for it nor act sad and contrite, as He has been portrayed, after all He was the Son of God.

If Jesus were as charismatic as He has been portrayed, there would have been sufficient voices to choose Jesus over Barabbas. When you read your Bible with an open mind, you will develop a new opinion of not only Jesus but most of the events as well. What I found was a man. He often referred to Himself as the Son of Man, who did not pursue infamy. He waited until He was twenty-nine to begin His calling to Be All He Knew Himself to be. He did seek disciples and speak in public, but it did not appear to be preplanned or that He had a desire to be either a public speaker or leader. He performed healings only when summoned or when a person in need was right in front of Him. In fact, most of His teachings sought to convey that as your True Self you will not be ill or confused. You would be aware of the Perfection that is your Created State of Being.

He preferred the company of drinkers and prostitutes as well as the local pub to the temples and priests. He did not attend family gatherings nor did He visit family on a regular basis. He was a FREE MAN who followed His inner voice, the voice of His true Father, and to do His Father's work. On more than one occasion Jesus avoided invitations, by today's standards He would have been considered 'anti-social.'

It seemed He did little that was 'expected of Him.' He did not yield a metal sword to divide people. He used the Sword of Truth to divide people from their delusions. He did not smite one's enemy. He saw no enemies, not even Pilate or Judas. At every opportunity He went alone to the mountains presumably to be in touch with Nature and His Father in order to rejuvenate, much as we still do today.

What does this Truth have to do with you? Jesus tried to explain time and time again that man is not victim to an angry judgmental God but master of his own choice, even down to Lazarus' dying. With all Jesus taught him Lazarus died because of his own lack of understanding, not a decision of God. The Scribes and Pharisees chose their behavior in the temple. The sales people knew they did not belong in God's house yet they made the choice to be there. Were they smote, as per Old Testament statements? No, they were taught their behavior would not be tolerated.

The Bible gives repeated stories of those who sow and those who reap. It is a fact if you plant wheat berries that is what grows. Wheat will grow and nothing else. Plant thistle, thistle comes up. If you plant anger, judgment, and wickedness don't expect to receive love and charity. No one is drawn to a growling, barking dog. It has nothing to do with God's judgment. It's what you personally choose. Buddhism refers to 'reaping what you sow' as Karma. Karma is nothing more than the notion, if you slap someone; it is very likely that someone will slap you. It is not always the person you slapped who slaps back, but sometime and somewhere, someone will probably slap you back. That's Karma.

Angry people are attracted to angry people. Peaceful people are drawn to peaceful people. Complainers and whiners are drawn to complainers and whiners. Successful people are drawn to successful people. However, people who falsely portray being peaceful will attract angry people. Jesus preached this over and over again in His talks and sermons. Who you are on the inside, in your heart, is what draws energy to you and determines the outcome of events.

Unfortunately the process of 'positive thinking' is not one-hundred percent as effective as we were once lead to believe. Although it has more merits than negative thinking, it is not even fifty percent effective. As long as our experiences and past patterning are not in harmony with our emotions, our hearts as Jesus said, *"cancel it out."*

> **Matt. 9:4 ASV** *'And Jesus knowing their thoughts said, Wherefore think ye evil in your hearts.'*

You cannot expect financial success if, deep within your heart or emotional structure you feel you do not deserve it. It is not that cut and dry. In order to achieve a higher rate of success and control over our lives we have to establish and understand thoughts and their action and where those thoughts have their origin. If it were that easy to create and attract good to you, then more people would be experiencing all the good in the world.

Chapter Three

MY OWN TRANSFORMATION

ALL PERSONAL HISTORIES TAKE A similar path in one way or another. From conception to death we go through the learning, loving, disappointment, suffering, and joys. Then life ebbs and we are given the gift of absolution in rebirth to evolve again. My life is no different.

In the spring of nineteen-seventy my life changed. There is no way I can truly convey the experience of these events, but I will try.

After my children left for school that morning I walked to the living room and looked out the picture window as I often did before the start of my day. I loved watching nature and the world around me. It always gave me a sense of well-being. But that did not happen this particular morning. The neighborhood I had known for more than half my life was gone. Instead, it appeared as though someone had taken an old black and white photograph of my neighborhood, blown it up and put the negative outside the window. What once were homes, trees, and 'tangible things' appeared to be opaque white, everything else was black as though it were the negative of a photograph and not the final print. I stared out the window waiting for the scene to return to what was familiar. I have no concept of the time I stood there, but the vision never changed. It has taken more than thirty years for me to develop even a semblance of understanding of what my eyes perceived.

At some point I walked away from the window trying to

comprehend what was happening. I headed toward my bedroom to get dressed but had to grab the wall as the most amazing sensation overtook every fiber of my being. I was completely overpowered with the awareness that every breath I took, every sensation of my body was immersed in a sense of unconditional love. It literally dropped me to my knees in tears of gratitude, love, and appreciation. The feeling was so overwhelming I felt my heart would burst, as this loving energy held, cherished, and nourished me. It ebbed and flowed through my entire body as I surrendered my body, soul, and mind to its total love and compassion. Time was incomprehensible; it could have been seconds or hours. I know only that my entire being was encased in unconditional love. This being or energy or whatever it was held me suspended in time and space. I have no idea how long I was suspended in that realm. It seemed like seconds and an eternity at the same time. The feeling was so powerful, it was almost impossible to breath.

I have no idea what happened the rest of the day. I can only assume I eventually returned to my feet and to some form of reality. I must have gotten dressed and carried on with my day, but I am certain I remained in some state of ecstasy and confusion as I tried to understand what had transpired. I can state unequivocally that my entire consciousness and awareness changed during that moment in time. In the 'twinkling of an eye' I had been changed from a young divorced woman with low self-esteem, no sense of security and no knowledge of whom or what I was. I found myself in a state of peaceful calm detached from problems or ill feelings of any kind. I felt strong and secure and more than anything else, I felt a peaceful sense of wisdom.

Previously, I drank too much even if it was mostly on weekends. I went from one bad relationship to another. I never felt loved or wanted and certainly felt totally incapable of being a mother. My life was riddled with health issues and I had had headaches and stomach problems since age eight. To say that I had little or no ability to make a good choice was an understatement.

I loved my children and did the best I knew how to raise them but my mothering skills were, at best, barely adequate.

After that I read every book I could on religion and spiritual experiences seeking some explanation of what had happened to me. My children would do their homework while I poured over book after book. When I asked a question, answers just came to me then I would find books that confirmed the answers I had received from an unexplainable source. I read the Bible a lot but the more I read the more questions I had. I would go to church, listen to Sunday school teachers and sermons only to come home with even more questions. That led me back to the library for even more books, which led to even more reading and even more questions. It was endless. The more I asked, the more I learned, the more I learned the more excited I became about the information I received. Nothing interested me except the search for Spiritual answers and caring for my children. Each new answer brought more peace and a greater sense of who and what I was as a human on this planet.

Parables, statements in the Bible, and lyrics in religious music that were once abstract phases suddenly became deep Spiritual messages. Like the old cliché, 'you can be changed in the twinkling of an eye,' I was changed. I no longer thought, felt, reasoned or reacted as I had the day before. I looked the same and probably most people saw the same old me, but at my deepest level I was a different person. I still feel tears well up in my soul when I hear songs that sing of the love and grace of God. You may think you know what I am describing, but until you have been transformed you can never truly know. I had been saved from my own mental and emotional hell and reborn into someone who was at peace and felt strong and secure.

Strangers would try to ask me questions and say peculiar things. But I knew what they really wanted and would answer the questions they had no words for. The strangers would be confused yet assured the answers they received were outside of me from a place where someone or something knew their soul. The accuracy of the response they received was so on target they could only accept it as the answer they needed and they were appeased.

My headaches and stomach problems were gone. I was physically and mentally strong. My children now had a mother who could guide them. Somewhere from within me came answers in the form of visions like panoramic movies that surpassed both time and space and be instantaneous. Each event would bring an indisputable new truth and awareness. I researched the responses and got nothing but confirmation of the facts shared within me. That still continues to this day. It is an amazing, enlightening and incomprehensible occurrence and certainly not something that anyone could understand unless they had experienced it themselves.

People were drawn to me like a magnet and as an attractive young woman men thought the attraction was romantic, but I knew where their true desire came from. One particular man was convinced that he wanted to spend his life with me even though we had nothing in common and no reason to spend time together. He was totally enamored and nothing I said would change his mind. He lived nearby and would always 'stop by' staying way too long. I kept hoping he would get bored and stop coming by.

I soon realized he was extremely bigoted and any mention of other ethnic races would infuriate him. We did not date, he just consistently 'dropped by' and stayed. In total exasperation one day I began talking about how much I enjoyed watching Sidney Poitier movies. He was livid. He said, "surely you can't tell me that HE is your favorite actor?!" I proceeded to explain that not only was he my favorite actor but I admired him greatly as a man and a human being. He blew up and left. I fortunately never saw him again. My point however, is that he was drawn to my energy but had no ability to realize it was different than what he normally felt when he saw a woman he wanted. I could sense exactly what was going on with him and no matter how hard I tried to reach out to his deeper being, all he was aware of was his own animalistic desires.

At that time I preferred being alone with my children and my studies. I had little desire to be outside of this learning, changing and Spiritual bubble. It captivated me to want to learn more, be more, and frankly, to serve God. I was convinced this was the state man was meant to be in. Simple needs were provided to me, like when I needed a bucket for work in the yard one would appear beside a road I was driving down. Little things were constantly available for me whenever I asked. I was too naïve and immature to realize I could ask for bigger things like great health and a good job. But back then I was just a baby learning how to walk in Spiritual awareness.

As I said, I understood people beyond their words and seemed to see into their souls. I saw them at their highest potential with their greatest abilities. When I looked in their eyes, I saw the God within them beyond their worldly state of survivalist nature. It was magical. My life was suddenly easy and uncomplicated. It had done a one-hundred-eighty degree shift from before that day I was dropped to my knees in total unconditional love. When I questioned my new state of being, why I was so different, the answer I received was clear; this was man's natural state of being.

I was not out of step, everyone else was. I was becoming what man was evolving into and eventually most people would live in this same consciousness. As eighteen months of this ecstasy passed it became clearer that this would become man's natural state of being and evolution. It was also made clear that there is an intelligence beyond human logic and reason that sees the world from the end result of where it started to where it is going. This intelligence was teaching me. I assumed it was God. I had no concept or reason to believe otherwise. But as I look back, knowing what I know now, it was definitely God because everything is God. As time progressed it was made clear to me that man has the ability to be in constant communication with this intelligence; that communication is the ultimate goal. Basically mankind would live as God/man or realization of God without separation.

So the questions changed for me. The question became, 'why me?' I was so blessed, so peaceful, so in control of my life. What I have conveyed is a mere glimpse of the life I really lived in that state of being. I became sad, because I had no idea why this had happened to me specifically. But more than anything I had no way of sharing this experience with others. I could only help one or two people achieve some deeper level of peace and love. And then there were the people I knew who told their children I was on drugs and to stay away from me. I had been very close to my local nieces and nephews prior to this event. I realize now our closeness came when a chauffeur or babysitter was needed. That was the first of many new heartbreaks for me.

As time passed I became aware of people who seemed to have experienced a similar transformation. They are teachers today such as Adyashanti, Eckhart Tolle, Wayne Dyer, Deepak Chopra, Krishna Das, and Ram Das to name a few. I read them voraciously. They provided exercises to help reach their same level of peace, love, and compassion but not one of them could explain exactly how they had each achieved their state of consciousness. Committed to share this process of evolution I reached out to God and said, "If this is real, I want to lose this connection and go back through the awakening to understand how it happened."

God was not quick to grant me my unconscionable wish but eventually He did and with that experience behind me I will issue this warning. Once you have attained a spiritual connection with this wisdom, as per the Bible, if you lose it or return to your previous state of consciousness, it will be worse than before. And believe me it was.

I will not go into detail of the months and years of darkness that followed. But I did suffer greater misery as a result of my own ignorance than I had before. As I called out to God I cried and wallowed in self-pity. I was angry and judgmental again. I became enmeshed with the same old people. I felt unloved and abandoned which was my inherited way of being. Basically my life became hell on earth. I had the teaching of others who achieved the state I so badly wanted back and did the recommended exercises, listened to their recordings, watched their videos, and read their books, but they never got me back to that state of communication and harmony. I did achieve a sense of peace and love. But not the connection to God nor the constant counsel of my questions. The clairaudience and clairvoyance was not there. And I had still not found a solid explanation of how their transformation occurred. The only stories that even closely resembled mine were cases of near death, except I did not see a tunnel or a light, and I lived this consciousness everyday not just the short time I was in that connected state of pure unconditional love. It had become my way of life.

This is where my story and a forty-five year journey really began, not with my awakening or rebirth, but at the moment of my return to being spiritually asleep. It started with one prayer I repeated to God until it was answered. The process took some time, but God answered as God does, "totally."

I will soon share my forty-five plus years' experience of downloading information to take you through **THE PROCESS TO RAISE YOUR AWARENNESS** without losing your mind. However, first I want to talk about the human download.

For the first time in history that we are aware of, we have a great parable to explain God. That is the computer, internet, and Cloud.

When we first became of aware that there was a God we were like the original computers. We were stand alone and connected to nothing. We could only receive information from other people, preachers, teachers, and family or friends. But the information we received was very limited and based on their filtered thought processes, limited information, and experiences. The original stand-alone computers were very similar in that they recorded limited information from the people who prepared the neat five and one-half inch floppy disks. These mostly held programs which make me chuckle today because that is what people try to do to others, program them into their way of thinking.

Then along came the neat smaller three and one-half inch disks. Computers were progressing and we could now save more information on the small disks then we could on the larger ones. Computer programmers were developing more versatile programs providing us with the ability to do more. So the more assistance we had the more we knew. But today we are more like the laptop and desktop computers. We don't have to be connected to the internet to use the computer. In other words, we can use the computer (the body), without being connected to the source, but it does not provide much for our day to day life. In fact, both are kind of purposeless and again limited without that connection to the internet or to God.

But God is real. God can be connected to. The Cloud is now within our communication space and is the collective unconscious. You can reach out to the Cloud or to the universe for information and assistance with what you want to do either on the computer or with your life. In other words, there is information directly from God but through a method of communication that is similar to the Cloud. It is stored there and you can download it once you find the right program in your head. Like the Cloud this universe or collective unconscious is filled with both desirable and undesirable information. It is up to you to search for the right information. When you get on the wrong page you just block it and go on. The collective unconscious is more viable than the Cloud because it has always existed, we just had nothing to use as an example to explain what this connection was.

Am I saying that God is nothing but a giant computer in the sky? Absolutely not, but I am saying the internet and Cloud have given us an example or parable of the hierarchy to communicating with God. We have to reach out to the internet, then the Cloud. We have to reach out to God. Like the internet, God does not come automatically connected YET. And the Cloud takes on another layer of communication. God's specialty is LOVE and helping. The collective unconscious/God Cloud is for answering questions and providing needed information.

Chapter Four

PERFECTION OF THE WORLD

C AN YOU EVEN IMAGINE A twenty-four year old woman, divorced, frightened and trying to raise four children alone with only a less than tenth grade education having this information in her head? And yet late at night I would still lay awake and wonder how I would be able to pay the bills, feed, and clothe my children when I was not getting any financial help from their father, an abusive man who made it a habit to threaten and torment me with his mother by his side. I have long forgiven him because you cannot begin to understand the teachings of Jesus without developing love even deeper in your heart. I knew he was very sick. Alcoholism is not a choice but a disease that affects the whole mind and body leaving the Christ within waiting for your healing.

When I received the following information I was in total shock and this may make you angry. It made me angry enough to challenge the information and insist on clarification. If you are in a difficult place mentally, physically, or emotionally this might be hard for you to hear but, the world is perfect as it is. Once you are able to perceive it as such you will understand

A) Man has total freedom of choice. It would not work otherwise nor have significance.

B) Its purpose/functionality is based upon man's evolution into God/man.

That does not mean man is **THE GOD.** It means man is to become the conscious co-creator of his own life. That is what made Jesus unique and classified as the first born Son of God. At birth, He came into this world knowing He was a fully conscious creator of His own life and lived under the law of total freedom of choice.

To become aware of your direct connection to God, or as some call it, Enlightenment, you don't have to eat the right foods, behave properly or even give up drinking. There is only one requirement and that is to have a burning desire beyond any other desires to make that connection. It can begin with questions like: Who am I? Why am I here? What is God? Who was Jesus, Mohammed, Buddha, etc.?

It is illogical to assume a person is born, lives, and dies to no ultimate conclusion except an accident of nature. If you observe the world around you everything has a purpose. One purpose or aspect is to build up, another is to tear down, but they are both for the same purpose, life. The entire evolutionary process is merely God's way of evolving a being to the level of God/man. To be clear, there is no name except the unknowable, for what we refer to as God. There is no accurate description, name or identity. So for the purpose of clarity I will simply refer to this entity as God.

The problem with the process of total evolution is that man has forgotten who or what he is as well as life's purpose. The physical manifestation continues its evolution but in the process humanity has been so busy evolving physically and mentally that it has bypassed the process of Spiritual Evolution. But in all Truth, the Spiritual aspect of our being has only been observing the evolution in preparation for the human body and mind to be capable of sustaining the power of the Spirit that has always been alive within man. However, most of us are unaware of that presence within.

Ultimately humanity will discover the human body, like a very advanced computer, can run without constant attention. The body does not require constant thought to breath, digest, pump the heart, etc. Allowing the body to maintain the systems it runs naturally will eventually leave the mind to simply live in an advanced form; creating life and enjoying every moment through connection to the ultimate source of life and wisdom. It is stated though that the road to this wisdom, knowledge, or connection is steep and narrow.

To help you understand why the "path" is referred to as steep and narrow I present some examples. The path is like a series of caves and though they appear as a straight line to the Supreme Being or Consciousness, it is a random path through many distractions, distractions not meant to be roadblocks or detours. Sometimes these paths seem like running a gauntlet but the gauntlet is to guide you not punish you. These distractions are just the simple process of experiencing, maturing, and growing; nothing more or less

In the beginning of the evolutionary process man is at his lowest vibrational energy. The main focus at this level is self-survival, self-pleasure, and self-aggrandizement which may manifest into addictions to deviant sexual behavior, drugs, alcohol, work, and recreation as well as criminal acts of murder, rape, robbery, etc. However, and we will address this later, do not think that all distractions are bad.

Most addictions or obsessions are a deeply engrained desire to return home, or so we think. We feel empty inside, unloved, unwanted, and unacknowledged for any worth or abilities. Beneath all these feelings is the one basic sense that God Himself has abandoned us. Even many successful people have these feelings buried within their psyche. They have just found a way to mood alter and continue in their successful careers. This sometimes leads to suicide because it can be difficult to understand the desire and what it really means, 'to go home.' It is what we call, God calling to awaken the Christ within you.

These examples are not about judgment, or proper or improper behavior. This is merely a way to show how easy it is to get sidetracked and help you avoid these pitfalls.

EXAMPLES OF DESTRACTIONS: (There is no significance to the order of presentation.)

- **Survival**: The need for food, comfort, and sustenance, the methods of how those things are acquired and how you survive physically. Finding yourself totally occupied with the pursuit of your own personal needs and requirements.
- **Education**: Being taught, whether in school, college or on-the-job training, and locked into that method or desire for learning with the exclusion of everything else.
- **Religion**: There is no perfect religion. God is not religious, He is non-sectarian. To be caught in a religion is a very difficult distraction because it is acceptable and you must continually study to make sense of what that religion emulates as total truth.
- **Relationships**: Marriage, raising children, involvement with other individuals. Without Spiritual maturity and awareness struggling in any relationship is time consuming. You become locked into getting your own needs met and trying to fill the needs of others with few natural tools to work with.
- **Addictions**: To substances, alcohol, street drugs, prescription drugs, work, play, self-pleasure, care-giving, etc. These activities give the illusion to pacify the 'longing for home' for a period of time but ultimately leaves you empty and wanting more.
- **Emotional Control Addiction**: The desire to control yourself, others, and circumstances is a genuine trap. To be one's self is the only fulfilling state of being. Control only keeps you further from yourself.

These are just some distractions. There are many more that will divert you from the need and innate desire to find the God that lives within you. It does not mean you stop participating in life or these activities. However, anything that <u>monopolizes</u> your time and thoughts, and keeps you, on 'auto pilot' thinking "this is where I belong," prevents you from evolving during that time. Ultimately, you belong in constant communication with that which you are; a loving parent, a worker with responsibilities, an avid hiker, etc., and at the same time you are able to become as Christ was, the deliberate, conscious creator of His Life. The difference between who we are today and who we will become is our own perception. Nothing more and nothing less.

Scribe these words into your mind, your heart, on your walls, wherever you will read and accept them:

YOU ARE CREATING YOUR LIFE WITH EVERY THOUGHT AND EMOTION THAT YOU THINK AND FEEL.

That is Jesus' main message for mankind. As I said before, this is about the process and nothing more. By learning who we are and reconnecting to our creator we become conscious deliberate creators of our own life.

How do we become reconnected? Jesus answered that question simply, "become like a little child." For such as these shall enter the Kingdom of God, and where is the Kingdom of God, they asked? The Kingdom of God is within. So within, we are connected to God. How do we achieve that? You must become like a child, and what does a child do? A child will drive you insane with questions until he gets answers and this is what I mean to become obsessed with being reborn. It is simple. When you are born of the body, you are born through a water birth. When born of the Spirit, you are crucified or your old mental and emotional turmoil dies and you are born into Spiritual Man in communication with God filled with total peace. This becomes a natural way of living. You may think you are speaking and hearing from channelers or entities from the collective unconsciousness, but there is only one entity and that is God in His many, many forms. But remember, there are pitfalls, 'distractions' to trap you and block your evolution into the Spiritual Man you are meant to be.

In seeking and asking like a child you will receive answers allowing the death of your old trappings to be reborn into the Spiritual Man that you are. If you question this go into the Bible and see how many times Jesus said, "now when I speak like this I am speaking as the son of man, but when I speak to you like this, I am speaking as the Son of God." He was aware that sometimes he moved out of that state of being. You will too, and you alone are accountable for your states of being just as Jesus was. How you represent yourself and how your life impacts others is also your responsibility. However, once you've reach the Perfected State of Evolution or 'day seven' there will be no moving out of that consciousness. It will be natural for those you are in contact with to be in direct communication with God as you now live in that advanced state of being.

I am not aware if all religions teach what the Bible says. I do know the status Jesus held and He was born knowing He was in control of His destiny and in communication with God. I want to discuss the TEN COMMANDMENTS, their message and purpose. First, they are suggestions of how to live a progressive life not about living a good or bad, right or wrong life. There is no judge of your behavior except by yourself. When you judge yourself or others you condemn your own self to that mental and emotional state and behavior. The Ten Commandments are statements identifying a Man who is born of the Spirit and dead to the distractions of the world.

Once you are born of the Spirit you no longer wish to participate in activities referenced in the Ten Commandments such as, why would you want another God?

Exodus 20:2-17 ASV '*I am Jehovah thy God, who brought thee out of the land of Egypt, out of the house of bondage. ³ Thou shalt have no other gods before me.*

⁴ Thou shalt not make unto thee a graven image, nor any likeness of anything that is in heaven above, or that is in the earth beneath, or that is in the water under the earth: ⁵ thou shalt not bow down thyself unto them, nor serve them; for I Jehovah thy God am a jealous God, visiting the iniquity of the fathers upon the children, upon the third and upon the fourth generation of them that hate me, ⁶ and showing loving kindness unto thousands of them that love me and keep my commandments.

⁷ Thou shalt not take the name of Jehovah thy God in vain; for Jehovah will not hold him guiltless that taketh his name in vain.

⁸ Remember the sabbath day, to keep it holy. ⁹ Six days shalt thou labor, and do all thy work; ¹⁰ but the seventh day is a sabbath unto Jehovah thy God: in it thou shalt not do any work, thou, nor thy son, nor thy daughter, thy man-servant, nor thy maid-servant, nor thy cattle, nor thy stranger that is within thy gates: ¹¹ for in six days Jehovah made heaven and earth, the sea, and all that in them is, and rested the seventh day: wherefore Jehovah blessed the sabbath day, and hallowed it.

¹² Honor thy father and thy mother, that thy days may be long in the land which Jehovah thy God giveth thee.

¹³ Thou shalt not kill.

¹⁴ Thou shalt not commit adultery.

¹⁵ Thou shalt not steal.

¹⁶ Thou shalt not bear false witness against thy neighbor.

¹⁷ Thou shalt not covet thy neighbor's house, thou shalt not covet thy neighbor's wife, nor his man-servant, nor his maid-servant, nor his ox, nor his ass, nor anything that is thy neighbor's.

Why would you be drawn to do any of these things once you are born of the Spirit, at total peace, filled with the Love of God, and see that everything is God? What could take you away from that awakened state of being, especially if you had others who supported you and helped strengthen you in that awareness and knowledge of who and what you are?

The most important thing I had to learn is that my awakening was to that of my true nature, what I was born to be. It was nothing special, nothing exceptional and nothing that should be considered out of the ordinary. Previously I was only aware that I was acting in the Natural State of Man. Again I must repeat, you are not judged or condemned by anything or anyone other than yourself. In that judgement you condemn yourself to a state of misery outside the Kingdom of Heaven far from the seventh day of creation.

We are here evolving and growing to a level of truly understanding what judgment and forgiveness is. When you place judgment on someone it is caused by a need to recognize those same qualities or lack of good qualities with yourself. To grow and heal, you need to understand how that person feels or felt. What made them who they have become? Acceptance and forgiveness can only truly be established through empathy for the pain, suffering, and ignorance that is responsible for the behavior or status you are judging. This is the meaning of repent. You need to revisit the event or feelings and view them from all perspectives in order to see the perfection of God within the events. Then, you will have truly repented.

There are two options of establishing this. Method one is the judgment process. This is accomplished by drawing similar experiences into your own life that the judged person has experienced. If you are wise, you can glean the truth from your own experience to correct your own behavior. You also need to establish an acceptance of the fact that people are a sum total of all they have experienced and learned. Behavior is nothing more and nothing less. Each of us live in the result of both learned behavior and how we are treated.

It is not our position to condemn or accept the behavior of others but continue outside of acceptance or condemnation. Both are a form of judgment and by doing so you put yourself in a position of determining what is right or wrong. There are two sides to every coin. To decide beauty is to determine others are not as beautiful. To determine perfection is to judge imperfection. When you begin to understand the perfection of life, you realize it is flawless. All action or behavior is equal because it is not the path one chooses in the process of evolving that is important, it is the end result of the individual's evolution that is the goal.

Forgiveness is a great secret of the soul because within that simple secret lie many keys to our own eternity. Judgment of course must precede forgiveness and is a major part of the act of forgiveness itself. To be free of judging means to be free of a need for forgiveness. I have heard many people state that they just cannot forgive a certain person or behavior.

My lesson for this came with understanding my mother's rejection of me. I won't go into the signs of her rejection, she just did, but she started pushing me away when I was eight years old. At thirty I went through the process of Hyper-sentience counseling for depression and it sent me into an evaluation of why my mother rejected me. I explored who my mother was and why she pushed me away while hugging and caressing others.

It dawned on me that my parents had never had a good relationship. Mother never felt she could totally depend on my father for emotional or financial support. More than that she was raised to believe men were the important part of the family, they were honored and revered whether that position was earned or not. In 1914, at the time of her birth and throughout her life, it was a stature given freely to men. Her mother died when my mother was only two, leaving her totally dependent on her father for everything outside of her own independence.

I was the youngest of six children and discovered my parents had a major fight during my mother's pregnancy with me. The fight basically came down to this final statement, "When this kid you are carrying leaves home, so will I." My father set into motion what is referred to as a postulate. That statement haunted my mother and when she looked at me I was a reminder that her husband would be leaving.

It didn't resonate with her until I was eight years old because her father had been there to offer support and comfort as he had done throughout her life. However, grandpa died when I was eight, that sense of security disappeared and the realization that when I left so would her only other sense of security. Understanding that I was a reminder my mother would lose her sense of security was exacerbated by the fact that I got married at sixteen. As I said, my father made a "postulate" by telling my mother he would leave when I left home but he did not know what he was setting into motion.

I intentionally got pregnant at fifteen. I was sixteen when I told my parents and got married. My father's indiscretions came to a head a few months before I left home the following April. My mother kicked <u>him</u> out of the house after I left. That was the "postulate." He left even though it was not his choice when the time came. It was not his plan but his words and emotions at the time he made the statement set his departure into action to fulfill that postulate, sixteen years later. This is another example of when we create our lives haphazardly how we eventually become conscious deliberate co-creators of our lives and events.

Chapter Five

GOOD ENOUGH FOR GOD

H AVE YOU EVER HEARD, "WE cannot be perfect or good enough for God?" This is religious propaganda, a way to control man. It was set into motion so long ago it has become a fact that keeps man steeped in fear. It is next to impossible to find a religion today that does not use fear as a way of controlling man. The need for this control is quite simple. If we knew how free we really were there would be no way of controlling mankind.

In studying the various religions of the world, there are two common themes. The first is man must strive to be good or he will never get to Heaven, Nirvana, Salvation, Samadhi, Valhalla, etc. The second is that man is a sinner and the only means to acquire the state of grace is simply by believing and "being good enough" to please God. God grants grace to those who "earn" it through their behavior and commitment.

Let's look first at the propaganda, "we must be good enough." The bible is filled with messages of "being good." The fact that man exists at all is by the grace of God. He was created in God's own image. God does not judge man. Man is perfect. These are fundamental Truths of existence. So what does being good enough mean?

We are encouraged to Not Serve Other Gods, Do Not Kill, Do Not Steal, etc. These are not commandments to anyone in the world today. They are old commandments and meant for man who does not and cannot know God. They were rules for survival. The yogi believes in the Law of Ahimsa. One must not lie, kill, or steal, but even the desire to do so should not exist in your heart. Jesus said the same thing:

> **Matt. 12:13 ASV** *'Ye offspring of vipers, how can ye, being evil, speak good things? for out of the abundance of the heart the mouth speaketh.'*

God gave man freedom of choice. With that freedom, man made his body dominant over his spiritual nature. You can never be good enough for God, because He does not judge anyone. We judge and condemn ourselves. Truthfully, it does not matter. You are either at a level of knowing who and what God is, or you are not. If not, you are subject to the Laws of Karma which means, do something bad and something bad will happen to you. Do something good and something good will be done to you. Christ stated this as, "what you sow, so shall you reap. You plant weeds, you get weeds. Plant wheat, you get wheat."

However, if you are aware of who and what God really is, then the state of being you live in is outside the law. This is simply because your state of being is one of not committing any acts harmful to others. There is no desire to do "wrong." Choice comes in the desire to find the whole self and cannot be found in self-discipline. How can you be "good enough" for a God who is total Love and does not judge you? What does being "good enough" mean when it has no meaning?

You are either with God, in a state of knowing who and what you are or, you are not. There is no in between. Until you reach the experiential truth that you are a Spiritual Being you will be reborn over and over again into a new body. Once reaching your full awakening you will become a being that inhabits a physical body which has access to all wisdom, knowledge, love, understanding, and compassion. You are total love, as God is.

God is an energy that thinks, feels, and creates. His love is total and pure to such a degree that if you felt it all the time it would become suffocating. Every fiber of your being is created out of total love. The glue that holds the universe together is energy; total love. That energy is God. The term "energy" is used loosely, because just as there is no accurate name for God other than the unknowable, there is no accurate description of what God is as to energy, frequency, fields, waves, particles, etc. When you develop this understanding, you will be as close as you can in your state of existence to know who and what God is.

Many believe they know and understand these concepts. They may have an intellectual knowing. However, if they had experiential knowledge of these facts, there would be no discussion at all. They would be living in a state that expounded all the so-called good qualities and would have no questions; they would just know all things.

To expand on this, delve into the various disciplines of yoga and Christianity. In yoga there are many types of disciplines such as total renunciation, obligatory works, dispassionate wisdom, love, and devotion. There is nothing WRONG with any of these disciplines, except that they are disciplines. Actually, they are attributes of a person who has moved into reality instead of Maya or illusion. We all live in the state of illusion. By this I mean, we are deluded into believing we are physical beings with a remote spiritual connection. The fact is we are totally spiritual but that is hidden from us in religion as well as the belief and practice of a life that is devoted to maintaining its physical misconception and irrational priorities.

Yoga also speaks of liberation, awakening, wisdom, independence, freedom, perfection, and extinction. Again, these are all natural attributes of the realized spiritual being. The term yoga means union with God. The true yogini, true students of yoga, seeks this union through many practices, meditation, physical asanas or postures, fasting, deprivation, and more. What they are in search of is Samadhi or Mahasamadhi, a state of ecstasy. Many yogis claim to have reached Mahasamadhi or union with God. If reached, this takes them totally out of consciousness with this world to live in some sort of euphoric exhilaration rarely communicating with others and incapable of maintaining the human body. There is no doubt that the experience of Mahasamadhi is real. However, they are trapped, just like the rest, in a lie. Why would there be a body if we were not to use it or be responsible for it. What kind of God would design a life only to negate all it represents? Samadhi is only a partial realization of who and what we are. Christians experience a type of Samadhi referred to as, "being born again," or "saved." Unfortunately, the Christians seem to believe this exonerates them from responsibility. They also experience a temporary state of spiritual ecstasy, but being unfamiliar with methods to maintain the ecstasy they tend to, as Christ stated, go back to their old ways.

Without fully understanding what they are experiencing it is difficult to comprehend what is actually taking place. And, once a person does reach the full state of reality, completely free of illusion, even if only on an intellectual or euphoria state, it becomes quite difficult to communicate what they are experiencing. Current terminology does not have adequate words to describe what they see, think and feel. Therefore, if anyone has a true connection to this state of being, they are restricted and limited by terms developed in a world that exists in the sixth day, at a level of illusion. These man-made limits are designed to keep you trapped in the illusion.

Sin is just an extension of the lie, "good enough for God." You are either in the now, living who you are, or you are in ignorance living by dogmatic rules in a society with religious laws that make it necessary for mankind to act inhuman.

Let's take "love" as an example.

We are made of love. It is what we want to have, what we want to experience, and what we are. Society today denigrates love. A common perception is, love is just a need for sex. But does sex satisfy the need for love? No, sex is not love; it is an instinctive act of procreation. Sex can be used as a method of conveying love, but it is not love, and love is not sex.

Man uses love as a tool to acquire what he believes he needs. It is a natural instinct to want to be loved; however, man has a misguided conception that this desire is based on love from another being. Often people mistake love for the desire to be wanted. Love in its purest form has no need to own, dominate, occupy, possess, or control. It is stated best here:

> **I Corinthians 13:1 ASV** *'If I speak with the tongues of men and of angels, but have not love, I am become sounding brass, or a clanging cymbal.'*

The description of love continues through verse thirteen.

Qualities of love express freedom for the object of your love. To have true feelings of love, you would encourage the object of your love to move forward in their own lives to create, grow, and achieve. Often, even with our own children, the feelings we define as love are simply an excuse to turn someone into who we want them to be. In much of current society, our latest version to prove the love for our children is to absolve them of any form of discipline for their actions. In fact, we are made to feel guilt and shame if we try to discipline our children in any way. Sadly, children without guidelines and discipline tend to feel unloved and overburdened. They lack a sense of security that is derived from the parent who is self-assured and secure enough in their wisdom to offer guidance and direction. Love is patient, encourages, and makes no demands of another. Identify the object of your love. Is that object, male or female, free to leave your life to seek a life for themselves or fulfill their own dreams? Does that thought leave you feeling threatened or fearful? Does it give you a sense of uneasiness? If so, it is not true love. It is your false belief that love requires the bonds of another.

It is our nature, as human beings, to desire the company

of likeminded individuals. The mistake we make is assuming that we love everyone we choose to be with. In fact, what we actually often feel is a fear of being alone or abandoned. The natural instinct is to want someone to help us with daily survival. Compatible partnerships are also a natural instinct. We do not wish to be so unique or different to risk isolation or loneliness.

If you take the general societal concept of love and dissect it, you will find it is a lie. Love itself has nothing to do with the feelings we attribute to the word. Take for instance this lie that has been told to children since the beginning of time. ALL PARENTS LOVE THEIR CHILDREN. It is only natural they love their children. Now explain to a child why some children are sexually assaulted and even killed by their own parents. At one time it was considered normal to kill off female babies because they were deemed to have no value in the family? They were not even fit to educate. How do you explain this to a child if all parents love their children? You do not. If you try you will only further confuse a child. By nature all animals, including humans, love their offspring. This, like all other societal lies, makes mankind what it is today. It is because of these "distractions" that mankind is divided from his natural state and understanding of who and what he is. Religion is a lie perpetrated upon man in order to restrain and control man. Religion is a byproduct of governmental agencies that have a need to control and regulate the activities of individuals to preserve the illusion that, for his own good, man needs to be controlled. Consider the government that ruled over the crucifixion of Christ. Was that not a desperate attempt to maintain control and fear?

Man, in his natural state, does not need controlling. If raised with the understanding of who he was and the power he possessed, he would not have any instincts to do things that needed to be controlled. Christ, through his teachings, tried to express that man could be just like Him.

It has been inferred by preachers that Christ spoke in coded parables to hide His wisdom and truth from those who were, "not worthy to hear the truth." Christ spoke in plain everyday language. He used parables as examples. They were stories of life in the time that He lived.

To explain this idea I have been trying to illustrate: "We live our lives today according to how society has designed us to be." An accurate parable might be to compare this to the same way we would say an astronaut utilizes his full training and potential by spending his life roller-skating.

Jesus did not speak in hidden messages and meanings. He was trying to tell people that nothing about life as they lived it was real. His message is still relevant to us today, as we remain in the sixth day of creation. Yes, we hurt, we bleed, we want, and need. But the fact is we do not have to. We have the power to acquire every want we could ever have. WHEN we understand who and what we are beyond all the lies we will be able to utilize these physical bodies and minds in their evolved state. We will be able to fulfill every dream and wish that mankind could ever conceive.

Chapter Six

FREEDOM OF CHOICE
CREATING YOUR LIFE

W E HAVE NOW ARRIVED AT the Garden of Eden. Many people ask, "Where did Cain and Able get their wives, or where did Lilith go?" But similar questions will just keep you at level six. The important questions are day seven questions.

What is the point of the Garden of Eden story? The object of that story is the freedom to choose is mankind's greatest gift. When the snake approached Eve had she been told not to eat from the tree of the knowledge of good and evil? God's one rule was to leave both of those trees alone. It was her choice to ignore the rule and taste the fruit. Then, in order to lessen her guilt she convinced Adam to take a bite right along with her assuring him it would be okay, and nothing would happen. Did Adam make a choice too? Of course.

How did God deal with their choices? This verse supports my observations:

> **Genesis 3:22 ASV** *'And Jehovah God said, 'Behold,* **the** *man is become as one* **of** *us, to know good and evil; and now, lest he put forth his hand, and take also* **of** **the tree of life***, and* **eat***, and live forever.'*

When examining this verse I find three things very interesting. Previous to this moment Adam and Eve had no knowledge of good or evil. And who was God talking to when he said, 'the man has become one of us'? By consuming fruit from the tree of knowledge of good and evil Adam and Eve became like Gods. And lastly, that man can live forever if he chooses. Most Christians know what happened next. God only chastised Adam but both were cast out of the garden. However, it was their own choice to eat the fruit and go against the rules of God.

The result of Adam and Eve's decision meant that man was given the freedom to live within a physical body, have a limited lifespan, and live a restricted existence. In other words, this choice traps mankind within the confines, needs, and demands of the physical body making him subject to the irrationalism of emotions, a maze of confusions, and frailties of the intellect. Since the beginning of man's creation he has locked himself into an action/reaction existence dominated by a flight-or-fight reality. And this brought about the need for laws and rules. Besides the Ten Commandments, there was one other law that God laid out for man, the Golden Rule, which we will discuss later

What does this gift of freedom of choice mean for us today? It is so all-encompassing that the only difference between "what you have and want" is your perception and understanding of "who and what you are." This includes your relationship to God. At this stage of evolution most of mankind believes that his abilities, wants and desires are limited and controlled. But man is only limited by himself and his beliefs. Man unknowingly thinks what he wants into existence with the haphazard support of his emotions. E equals energy in the term e-motions and it means energy in motion. What you think or desire requires that emotions set forth energy in order to manifest your thoughts into reality. As long as you are thinking, you are choosing your lifestyle, which means, you are doing that pretty much every moment of everyday.

I realized our thoughts were creating our lives but, like most people, I didn't understand just how powerful our thoughts were until I found myself in the "place of my thoughts." These were not casual thoughts, they were intense and serious. For many years I wanted very much to be alone and independent, with a job, a maid, and cook. I wanted time to write and heal. Then one day at age forty-four, I found myself with a new job. I remember standing in front of the employment office at a private base looking out over a dry lake bed. Other than the work camp there was no house, office or civilization except for our living quarters, about seven miles away, and a few guard stations to make sure you did not enter the wrong areas.

While waiting for my ride to take me to meet my bosses and see my work area I started chuckling. I realized I would not have to make my bed, clean my room, or cook. I just had to work, and sleep; the rest of the time was my own. I said to myself, "Girl, you wanted it you got it." It was exactly what I had been wanting and it was over fifteen hundred miles from home. I did not regret it; I embraced it and said, "Let's see what I can accomplish." I knew we were creating our lives, but until that moment, did not know how thoroughly we were orchestrating our own lives. This realization made me look for evidence of others getting what they wanted or feared, or to put it more simply, getting what they thought about. With time the facts became obvious. We manifest at the same rate as our vibrational frequency.

These are some of my observations: Elvis Presley was very afraid he would die young and he did. An article by Lisa Marie Presley stated that Michael Jackson talked a lot about a fear that he would die the way Elvis Presley died. He died at about the same age, also from drugs.

Our fears are like magnets pulling us to the object of our fear such as car accidents, losing a loved one, getting fired from a job, or being abandoned by a lover. Take a close look at your fears, turn them over to God, and tell Him they are not your fears anymore. Own that thought and repeat the process until that fear is completely gone. If you surrender to your fear, it will always be yours.

Other evidence of creating one's own destiny I observed was of childhood stars. Back in the fifties and sixties it was an advantage for a child star to remain small to continue their career. Mickey Rooney grew to be only five feet two inches tall and was able pass as a child star into his twenties. Judy Garland at her tallest was four foot eleven; Natalie Wood was only five feet tall, Shirley Temple was five feet two inches; and Jerry Mathers topped out at five foot seven. You can see the pattern. These actors had lucrative careers as children but there were no guarantees that they would continue their successful careers once they reached adulthood. It's not hard to imagine they heard things like; "Don't outgrow this role," "I hope you don't start growing during this season," "Cross your fingers you'll be available next season for this role but you can't grow an inch and don't let your voice change." I imagine their agents were not shy about expressing their own fears when it came to business.

So, what is the best approach to looking at your life and accepting it is what you have chosen? And how do you create what you really want in your life? Let me share a story.

While I was on that military base camp as a civilian employee there were fifty men to each female. While the majority of these men were not necessarily the most desirable people you would want to know, there were a few. Many were married and looking for fun, but the same was true of the women. I had a short relationship with one of these men and it was horrible. During my long three hour drive back to my main residence for the weekend it occurred to me that this man was exactly what I had asked for BUT I had only asked for a few things. I wanted to meet a man who was an Aquarius, tall, nice looking and loved the outdoors. I should have added that this man be sober, a non-smoker, and at least nice.

I thought, "How about asking for everything I really want

in a companion, not necessarily a marriage partner but someone who shares the things I enjoy." So I began thinking of my list, this time being thorough, and specific. I wanted tall, blond, of German descent, a non-smoker, not much of a drinker, a man who loved the outdoors, and so on. It was a long list; after all, my drive was three hours alone with nothing else to occupy my mind. Two weeks later he appeared, but God always provides better than you request. That was thirty-two years ago and I cannot begin to express what a wonderful relationship we have. And yes, he is tall, blond, and of German descent.

But it gets even better. I wanted someone who was a blue collar worker, and worked with his hands, Of course that is mostly who I meet at the camp, but ten years after we met he became an Information Technology Administrator which, of course, is working with computers. About five years after he changed professions I got a chuckle because I realized that when I first started my writing, which not only meant writing, but also researching my questions about God and religion in general, this required working a lot on a computer, something new to me. I wanted to be married to a computer expert. At that time, I was right where I requested to be. Once again, I got more than I hoped for.

God is mindful of my needs, not because I am special. I have been refining my discovery that we are the creators of our universe. Let's look at you. Are you happy and content? What is missing in your life? What would you change? What are your goals? Now, let's look at what might be holding you back. Do you have low self-esteem? I did and still get hit with attacks of unworthiness. Don't fixate on the negatives in your life. If you have low self-esteem, accept it and turn it over to God, take a deep breath and know who you are. Remember, "The only difference between what you have and what you want is your own personal perception of who and what you are." Put that on your mirror. You are a Spiritual Being having a human experience; you are a child of God. And that God says you are also a God. Change your perception to be in line with your new knowledge of yourself. It is attainable but only with perseverance and something you need to work on each day.

Emotional baggage is another stumbling block preventing us from being free. Science is on the verge of verifying that emotional baggage does not only come from personal experiences but it is also in your genes. With this information I can now understand that not only were my abandonment issues just perceptions I created from my experiences during childhood but has also been programmed into my genes via generations of behavioral patterns. Wonderful, you may be thinking, now I need to fix my genes. Nope, you don't. Just accept the role it plays in how you feel and recognize it is a genetic illusion. It may not be your issue but someone else's.

I have another truth bomb for you. Your physical and emotional feelings may not even belong to you or have anything to do with you. There are many empaths or very sensitive people who pick up on the feelings of others and take them into their own body. People with this trait pick up on emotions that others are going through. If you can sense when someone is going to call or that someone is in need of you, you are most likely picking up on their energy fields. If this is you, it would be beneficial to find a book on protecting your energy field and setting your boundaries.

Now, back to genetics. Psychological patterns forced upon people can change their DNA and that DNA is passed to future generations. Pedophilia is actually encouraged in some societies today. What is your ethnic generational gene pool filled with? All these things affect our self-worth, our ability to be strong and move forward. So, when you add the influence from chemicals and genetics, how many thoughts do you really have in choosing what you create each day?

To begin to achieve the goal of a controlled and directed co-creator you must first understand that "emotions generate energy," and "emotions are the energy that moves your thoughts into action." Emotional baggage is the main weakness in attaining the power of positive thinking. Imagine this; "I will have a new car." "I deserve a new car." "My new car is here, now." BUT your emotional and self-esteem training says, "Fat chance, buddy." "Who do you think you are?" Our emotions, if negative, negate the positive thought and the new car does not arrive. Ask yourself what you have manifested inside that is canceling what you want.

Also consider the vibrational rate at which you currently vibrate. If you are suffering from any of the previously mentioned chemical and emotional issues, it is difficult to have a high or rapid vibrational rate. The higher your vibrational rate the faster you manifest your desires. So, even if you are able to keep your thoughts and emotions focused and positive there will be a time delay in manifesting your wishes and desires.

Unfortunately, there is no overnight, instant formula for getting past our buried, emotional trauma. I, personally, am filled with a sense of unworthiness and abandonment issues. There are valid reasons to have them, but I have made a choice to move beyond those feelings by following some basic guidelines like; people are often removed from our lives for a reason, don't chase after them. Or, you do not have to remain in an abusive relationship no matter who that person is. I feel it is part of our own evolution to move on from these relationships and realize they are preventing us from living to our own potential. You have to stop judging to stop being entrapped within judgment. If you judge others you are judging and condemning yourself. We cannot just live our lives saying, I have to be more loving and compassionate. Human beings are complex. We have to deal with our belief systems and decide who we chose to spend our lives with as well as how we think and feel toward others.

Before moving on we have to go back to forgiveness. There are many people today who publicly state they cannot forgive, yet profess to be Spiritual people. And there are also people who say they forgive but if mentioning the ones forgiven, these people often have a very negative response. When forgiveness is valid and complete you feel love and compassion for the one who initially made you upset or angry. Often when people behave badly it is because of their genetic programming and emotional baggage just as your behavior is based on the past. In order to forgive you need to develop some understand of who that offending person is.

To understand their behavior you need to look at their past. Most likely you have triggered a negative feeling from their past. Once you see their reaction as something coming from their own damages and needs you can begin to forgive them because you have your own memories of pain and suffering. Like you, they are damaged and in need of healing. But perhaps you have reached a level where you can have compassion that they are still trapped inside their own damaged past while you are breaking free from old patterned behavior.

It is time to discuss collective consciousness. Since there is a "collective unconscious," it stands to reason there is a "collective consciousness." The "collective unconscious" is literally a collective of all thoughts coming from an unconscious or unaware realm; therefore, "collective consciousness" is the collective thought becoming conscious or aware of the chaos being created by the unconscious thoughts of all people throughout the world. So, what does that actually mean?

As an example, there are many people who devote a lot of time, energy and thought into jet fighters. They absolutely love them. As children they had airplane toys and now they prefer the real thing. They read about them, dream about being in one, and have discussions about them. They have visual images expressing their interest all over their house. In order to have a need for jet fighters, we must have war. In order to miss the camaraderie of being with soldiers we must have a need for soldiers and/or war. If one hates other races, people, and religious groups, judging and condemning them, then that is reason for war. You can see where

I am going with this. Our thoughts affect group consciousness and collective energy because we are all as one.

Video games need to be addressed because there is so much controversy about them. They are a double edged sword. On the one hand they promote violence but if used properly, which is rare, they can promote peace. Use them as a tool to release suppressed anger, violence, hate, and retaliation to help move beyond these feelings. Learn to use it as a means for developing controlled and useful motor skills. When you are finished with the games take a deep breath and release yourself of anger and tension. Make a conscious commitment to send out peace, love, and acceptance of yourself and others. This does not mean we have to stop being joyous, but we do have to stop inflicting unintentional violence on others through our desire to challenge ourselves to a simple video game, otherwise, we hold onto these feelings then release them in anger, violence, and war or mass murder.

If you know a teen on drugs understand that the drugs and medications only exacerbate their feelings of hate and inadequacy. Reach out to the family. Help them search for better solutions. Assist them in finding therapists who promote love-of-self and life, and can help them come to terms with their sense of inadequacy. In order to evolve we have to find a method, not of interfering in the lives of others, but assist in resolving situations they feel trapped in. It is hard to see your way out of a dense jungle but people who have already navigated a jungle can help you find your way out. Sadly, many of these drugs come from the so-called "trained medical world." At the end of the day we have to be responsible for what we put in our bodies and help those who are already subjected to harmful drugs. It is a fine line to walk but when we reach out, love, and care for each other we lift the vibration and eventually the negative and hate will be replaced not only by love and compassion, but joy and peace as well.

Again, if you can sense when someone needs you or wants to talk that interconnectedness continues through all levels of life. It does not stop because you are aware of the one person; it stretches across all of humanity. Mass creating is all around us at all times. It's everywhere the mind goes; the passion is, in what we seek, and what we want. These thoughts paint a picture of the future not only in your life, but in the lives of the entire world and universe.

There are men and women who fantasize about extra marital affairs or forcing another into sex by physically or psychologically maneuvering them or in some cases with the help of a drug. Others get angry and think about how they would like to commit violence against a person, company, or group. The games your own mind play are endless but thoughts become a piece of the collective of negative thoughts and consciousness. You may wake up in the morning and miraculously have forgotten that thought of committing violence you had the night before but that thought, like a cloud forming into a storm, now has its own life. Like the serene cloud that seems to be peacefully floating in the sky, soon other clouds form and join it. The next thing you know a storm is on its way with the potential to become a tornado. You did not act out on the thought but you gave birth to the thought which then takes on a life of its own.

Just as people can reach out to the collective unconscious and discover creative information as Steve Jobs publicly claimed he did, others can find negative support for their destructive action in the same manner. There are stories of young people being administered anti-psychotic drugs the medical community has tested and are known to sometimes take the patient into homicidal thoughts. But yet they continue to prescribe these drugs on the pretense that they will "help" them blend into society. However, some of these people move into a deeper anger and depression wanting to hurt others to stop their own pain. Like the cloud floating in the sky it looks harmless until it attracts the "living energy" of depression and anger. And this tornado, which is made from the pieces of his background and knowledge of guns, swirls into murder. Our thoughts, desires, and goals are a part of the collective whether positive or negative. There is no regulator that says this thought can take on energy and this one can't. If it is thought it becomes energy in one form or another. Pay attention to your thoughts.

One day I asked the collective unconscious this question. Is God the same thing as collective positive thought and is Satan the combination of negative thought? The download or answer came very quickly. "I (God) was there in all three of your serious accidents and you came out with just a scratch. But all three cars were destroyed. I was there the myriad of times you almost died or was given a life ending diagnosis and yet the disease dissipated. I was in the hallway with you that day and I am here now. What do you think?" And I KNEW experientially that there was a very real definite difference between the collective unconscious and what we refer to as God.

Jesus was adamant about this verse being the most important.

> *Matthew 22:36-40 ASV 'Teacher, which is the great commandment in the law? [37] And he said unto him, [n] Thou shalt love the Lord thy God with all thy heart, and with all thy soul, and with all thy mind. [38] This is the great and first commandment. [39] [o] And a second like unto it is this, [p] Thou shalt love thy neighbor as thyself. [40] On these two commandments the whole law hangeth, and the prophets.'*

The fact is, we keep the second commandments perfectly. We do love our neighbors as we love ourselves because there are very few of us that truly love ourselves.

The commandment is this:

> *Matthew 22:37 ASV 'Love the Lord THY God with all thy heart, and with all thy soul and with all thy mind.'*

Jesus did NOT say Love **the** Lord **the** God. When he said **thy** heart he meant **your** heart. When he said **thy** soul, he meant **your** soul. When he said **thy** mind, he meant **your** mind. And when he said "**Thy** God," he meant the God that lives within you. I have never met anyone who understands the true meaning of these verses. It is easy to love an abstract God outside of one's self. You must accept that there is a God within you before you can love the Lord Thy God. Not many people really like their human self so imagine what a challenge it is to love the Lord God within that you don't even believe exists. Can you accept there is a Lord God within you? You must come to terms with that very God before you can master the rest because, as Jesus said, the **whole** law and the **prophets** hang on this one commandment, just everything hangs on these two commandments. Let's read that again. The whole law and the prophets hang on those two commandments. Those are the only two commandments Jesus gave to humanity and the world. EVERYTHING relies on those two commandments. Please do not continue until you understand this or have ears to hear it. Open your minds and absorb the complete meaning of what was given to man. Love the Lord thy God with all thy heart, and with all thy soul, and with all thy mind. And love your neighbor the same way you love the Lord your God within and know that they have God within them also.

Come to terms with the fact that you are a God. Love yourself. Love others in the same way by forgiving yourself, forgiving those you feel have wronged you, release and heal the past, begin the process of love and develop a pattern of thinking compassionately. As this process comes to fruition, your vibrational rate will increase and over time you will be able to attract your desirable thoughts and words more rapidly. As other people evolve and develop these behaviors the sooner we will evolve into a Conscious Co-Creator of the Life the Lord our God deserves.

Chapter Seven

REINCARNATION AND CHOOSING YOUR NEXT LIFE

To BE CLEAR, I AM not a channeler, seer, mystic, or anything other than a person with recall of several lifetimes, including the first time I entered a body. There are people who receive information from what has been named the Collective Unconscious and more recently called the Cosmic Consciousness. This same energy is now being researched and called the Morphic Resonance. It is important to know that thoughts are energy and have a life of their own. Not all information received comes from a positive, helpful entity. It is our job to discern the energy sharing information. Also, not all energy is from deceased individuals but a collection of thoughts of both those living and dead. Thoughts are energy and they continue even to those who are not aware of this. Science has discovered an electromagnetic field that moves around the earth in a stream. It has been perceived this field is actually the collective thought of all those who have passed through human form or are still living. There is a huge possibility part of the information comes from entities that have never been in human form at all. When individuals think of new methods of accomplishing a task or new inventions, it often occurs to more than one person. Thoughts are interconnected. In fact, the same thoughts often occur to many people at once. Some will take action and do something with the thoughts. More than likely one will make and manufacture the new idea. That is why you hear people say, "I thought of that years ago." They probably did, but they did not act on it. The recorded inventor did.

Through the eight lifetimes I recall, there is a similar theme of events over and over again like a Star Trek version of the "Conundrum." In these lifetimes I held knowledge I continue to have today but have repeatedly refused to share. I judged no one would accept or understand the information I received from this Consciousness. My purpose, in this lifetime is to stop repeating the same scenario. It has been made clear to me if I do not convey what I know in writing or public speaking I will have to return to an even worse life, over and over again, until I "fess up," or share with the world, or whoever has the ears to hear what I KNOW to be true. So I am complying.

I have come to understand why I am in a human form, why I am here, what my objective is, and what I must do. I have strong recall of a few of my previous lives, and we all have previous lives. Within that knowing is an understanding of why things occur such as murderers, pedophiles, birth defects, etc. Never doubt that this world is perfect as it is. You may not approve of the way it works, why things are the way they are, but by the time you finish this book you will have a stronger understanding of the perfection that exists. It works. We just do not totally understand it. Everything that happens in this life is for one purpose and that is for you to evolve to perfection. I am one of the many who has been given the responsibility to teach how this world works and help you develop an understanding that nothing in your life is 'inflicted' upon you.

Let's look at current human behavior, where it comes from in our past and how it manifests in our present. It is important we accept the purpose of current religious institutions and what their future purpose will be. We will also address preparing for absolution and your return to another human body. In a minor way we will examine misdirection to help mankind understand that, "This world is absolutely perfect as it is," whether you approve of the method or not.

Remember, this is downloaded information and not just my words and memories. I want to share a story to reassure you that these memories don't have to devastate your life. My first memory of life is probably a little different than yours. I remember looking down upon primordial ooze that was very similar to the Discovery Channel computer graphics of what science perceived it to be. I saw a little fish swimming lazily around seemingly having a nice mellow day. I was observing it from a 'state of consciousness without actual form.' It looked like fun so I moved my awareness, my consciousness, into the body of this sweet little fishy. Immediately, along came a big fish and the little fish was in its mouth. However, I had the ability to instantly jump back out of the little fishy, but the fish's body did not. It was consumed by the big fish. The lesson was pretty simple. Next time choose the big fish. It was also obvious that I could leave the body before pain and suffering was inflicted upon the fish. Remembering past lives can be that unremarkable, but if observed as though you were watching someone else's life, its purpose may be revealed. Within each of these lives there is a continuity that will clarify who you are. In all actuality there is no proof the life you recall is 'your personal past life,' or just one brought by the collective consciousness to help fulfill your evolutionary path. These memories are shared to set you free of all restrictions.

Hopefully by now it is clear why we need to accept responsible for our own thoughts, actions, and emotions. We must be like the watchman at the gate standing guard to prevent any thoughts that might bring harm your way. Ironically, the harm is your own thoughts and feelings. We must discipline our mind and emotions to release all feelings of separation and pain because this is where depression and violence breeds. Dealing with our past honestly and repainting our views of how we have been harmed will take us to a place of love and peace we have never known before; a return to our real home.

At one time or another, many of us have overheard someone say they are ready to die. They are ready to go to Heaven, or stop the pain and suffering, or just ready to surrender to the struggle to remain alive. They will be glad when it is over. It was made clear to me thinking along those lines will get you nowhere. Being in the physical body is where our future lies. God did not create a body for man to just discard when he was tired of it. That is why we are here. That is why we have a physical body. There are some people who think God made a mistake when he created a physical human being. According to many religions, the moment God created a physical body he handed out a myriad of orders that said you can't use it for anything enjoyable. Dying is all you should look forward to so you can go to the place of peace and love. The human physical form was created as a vehicle for God to experience love, life, laughter, enjoyment, and evolution. The human form is to enjoy life, dream, create, celebrate, be limitless, and ascend to the heights right here on this planet. So, don't believe that when God created the human form he said no fair using it. Use it joyously with love and respect.

The body is so important He gives us a new one every time we destroy this one. Reincarnation is a gift of the human body from God. Keep an open mind as we must look at the lies involved with reincarnation. Death is something we all want to avoid, but have you looked at the ramifications of eternal life in one body using the same methods of life that we use now? Imagine you are three-hundred-and-twenty years old and have accumulated money or whatever method of exchange is available. You have approximately twenty-two generations of descendants and one of those descendants is standing in front of you. The story they share is of neediness and desperation they want you to pay their way out of this. Or maybe this descendant is having a birthday party or wedding. How much of yourself will you be able to share with each generation? What will your responsibility to them be? But that's not even the main point, this example is just one of reality expectations.

What is real is that death and rebirth are the greatest absolution of sin, Karma, or whatever you call the mistakes of your past. For most, but not all, dying is an event that presents you with the opportunity to drop habitual behaviors, anger, wanting, self-pity, abuse, and so on. You go to a place like a purgatory but you are not forced to stay there. It is a place of introspection where you are given the opportunity to look at destructive behaviors from your past as well as the opportunity to release and move beyond them. You are not forced to stay for any period of time. It is choice and it is opportunity. Not everyone chooses that path. If you do choose to release the negative behavior then you will receive a new body with that portion of your frequency released in absolution. You can, by perpetuating similar behaviors, draw that same destructive pattern back into your life. But your new body comes free of that label. Most people are reborn into a clean slate and it is their choice what they do about it. But it is more complicated than that.

Many religions teach reincarnation. Christianity once taught and believed in it. Twenty-five percent of Christians believe in reincarnation today despite the fact that in three-hundred-and-twenty-five AD Constantine forced Christianity to stop its teachings. Punishment for discussing reincarnation was beheading, a pretty effective law. This is why reincarnation is not included as part of the Bible or Christian teachings.

As previously stated, I currently remember only the lifetimes that teach my purpose for this particular lifetime. The wisdom of creation is such that the past lives I currently remember only relate to my responsibility here. It would be insane to have all memories of each lifetime consistently in our conscious mind. Presently, I have no purpose for remembering missing lifetimes which is why we were given the gift of forgetfulness, and it's a monumental gift. The time is coming when the veil of forgetfulness will pass and the memories will be here for all. At that point we will have evolved enough to accept the memories and past without those events overshadowing our life journey. I have known and shared this fact for years. There are many stories of children who remember past lives and their parents who encourage these memories to help them achieve a better quality of life.

Change is happening. If you choose not to be a part of it that's ok, because your time will come when you least expect it. If you choose to be a part of it I may have something that will speak to your heart, or at least to your soul, regarding the many lives you have lived.

A person comes into this world as who they have always been. The being enters the womb as an eternal being wrought with lessons to learn, motivation to achieve, and evolution to continue. There is much to learn about this seemingly simple process of natural, instinctive procreation. It is difficult to know where to start. How often do we hear "how can those children be so different when they have the same parents and are treated exactly the same?"

Again, each child is who they have always been. When an entity is drawn to the womb they come with a vibrational rate which includes DNA, genetics, level of evolution, and a predetermined vibrational attitude that they carry with them. We refer to it as the soul. The soul only changes through choice and evolution. The real question should be, why did that being come through these parents with this family? Each individual being consists of an electromagnetic signature; this is what was previously referred to as frequency. Electromagnetic is not an exact terminology of the field consisting of the being that enters the womb. It is actually a composite of electromagnetic, energy, ethereal, and elements we have not yet learned or manufactured a label for. This field carries experiential, physical, emotional, and intellectual markers that are drawn into the fertilized egg which has a similar, but not perfect, match to the parents at the moment of conception. The vibrational field of the parents is based on the same criteria, however, can be influenced by "the mood of the moment" which is determined by many factors. Are the future parents, at the moment of conception, under the influence of any mental or emotionally altering chemicals such as alcohol or drugs? The parents could be fighting, having make up sex, be "just in the heat of the moment, struggling with an inability to conceive, or of course, fear of getting pregnant. By the grace of God, they could even be enjoying a loving time together. But the point remains, the physical, mental or emotional state they were in at the moment of conception will attract an individually matching frequency or electro-magnetic field. The parents-to-be may or may not be experiencing their normal day-to-day frequency but, the newly returning entity will be drawn to the vibrational rate they are currently generating. This is why children are individuals and not clones of each other. This is also why their behavior, abilities, and interests are unique. Like magnets being drawn together, the entity is attracted out of the ethereal and into the womb by the similar vibrational rate of the moment.

I don't use astrology to determine my life's influence and direction, but I am convinced that astrological signs do influence both positive and negative personality traits. The planets, stars, and moon change position constantly. Their rate of vibration and gravity affects each of us in different ways. It also influences personality, interests, and compatibility. The time is past due for family planning counseling to include the time of conception, and time of birth as a compatibility guideline between the parent's births signs and the child they are planning for. It would make parenthood a lot easier for all involved.

Another concern regarding reincarnation is the death penalty. When I look at all the violence around the world today, I frequently ask, is this the rebirth of Jeffrey Dahmer or some other mass murder that died through the death penalty or other violence? It certainly stands to reason that once born they can easily revert to previous activities. The point I want to make is, there do exist entities which, for one reason or another, are extremely anxious to return to human form to continue their activities. Often this is for a continuation of anger and violence but it can also happen because of artistic abilities, humanitarian goals, or other strong desires. In those instances they can force their energy into a set of parents who are having haphazard sex, where there is no commitment and their frequency is on a very low scale. It could come out of a one-night-stand or any relationship with no commitment.

I know I am repeating myself, but it's all based on frequency and/or electromagnetic fields. What establishes those fields? To name a few; thoughts, desires, goals, actions, and attitudes establish the frequency of those fields. When you ask why those parents have a child with this dreadful disease or another deficiency, you have to look at all aspects. Most of the time that question is rhetorical. But to develop an understanding to a similar question may help you understand your own life situations. In the observations, it will illustrate how much power you have and guide you to make better choices for your own life. When born into human form we come with our own frequency, one that has been established throughout our own incarnations. Our basic memory, attitude, personality, and even physical health follow us throughout our soul incarnations. Who we think we are is carried lifetime after lifetime in the soul.

What DNA, traits, and habits determine the frequency for our rebirth? I have already mentioned attitude and talent but everything about this life begins to formulate the frequency for rebirth. Being in an accident could be a fear you have, but that fear could come from an accident in a previous life. This accident could even be a repeat of the same physical damage from a previous life, such as loss of a limb. We would be born with the limb then lose it long before we leave the physical body, but the imprint and way of life is on the soul. The frequency can come from resentment or judgement of another that you take with you. You might carry resentment of your parents through to your death while they carry the hurt that you have abandoned them. So the frequency itself could be the energy that now allows you to become their parent in a next life.

Without clarity of thoughts and feelings people who deeply love each other and remain friends and companions throughout a lifetime, or if you simply long to reestablish a connection with another person; your frequency could bring you together as brother and sister. However, you could retain the previous desires of intimacy for each other and create the taboo of incest in this lifetime. This is why the truth can set you free. If you suffer from guilt over incest in this lifetime and look at this as the underlying cause, then maybe you can more readily forgive and accept the event for what it is. You can also appreciate and accept the bond you feel with each other without guilt and without the need to act upon that feeling. So you have to be clear that you do not want to be together in an improper relationship or that you wanted to meet and become life partners again in the next life.

A similar scenario can be true of pedophiles. Let's look back at the history of adults having sex with children without judgment and disgust, keeping the frequency and collective consciousness in mind. It was a more primitive time and life was much different than our lives today. Only in the last one hundred years have we begun to develop self-help groups and books that teach us to be more caring and humane. At one time, young boys were taken to battle with soldiers to use for sex in order to build their testosterone, or so they said, to be fiercer on the battlefield. And girls, those girls who were considered useless to the family, could be sold for sex or slaves, or be thrown on the burial pyre with owners and rulers who used them as concubines. And they could be murdered just for being girls. Children were property, as were wives, and not that long ago especially when you look back at the number of lifetimes you may have lived.

Then there was the attitude of rulers to marry brothers and sisters in order to retain family control over a country, even fathers to daughters and mothers to sons. When looking back on previous lifestyles and attitudes, what was once acceptable, normal behavior is now considered illegal and disgusting. Look at sports and war, we teach our young to fight for sport in the name of entertainment. We send them off to fight and kill in wars then wonder where all this hate and anger come from. It makes me want to scream at our schools and at our political leaders. Let's open our eyes and be honest about the violence in our country. Violence and compassion are taught with the same mouth and we expect our children not to be confused or engage in violence. If violence is already in their past frequencies, then it is just reinforced and triggered by our attitude. No one knows where that violence will surface. It's time to reevaluate what we accept as normal. How people can watch boxing with all that verbal banter before the match and not see what it is teaching our youth? Who would not love to leave their poverty-filled life for the charmed lives of professional boxers, wrestlers, or others in combat sports?

Sadly, I am not surprised when I see a professional football player has been arrested for domestic violence, dog fighting, losing their temper in public, or even killing another. Think about what is being programmed into their heads by the coaches. It's the same violence inflicted on young boys forced into battle with the soldiers in the middle ages. When words like, "attack, harm, take him down," etc. is hurled at them day after day under pressure to perform, what do you expect? You condition their testosterone to run at its peak then say, be calm and loving at the same time. This is the programming we live with. If you are skeptical of this then ask yourself why seemingly nice people can sometimes go berserk fighting and killing, and will even join ISIS to act out their feelings. It is a programmed frequency. We need to realize what we are doing to ourselves and others. We need to take our power back.

We can start by understanding what the soul is. The soul is the keeper of your unique entity. It is your "baggage" and travels throughout your incarnations to reassemble what makes you – it is your memories, basic personality, attitude, and physical health. It also carries your interests and desires. This is why children come into human form with talents and skills already intact, like prolific pianists, painters, and singers. There are toddlers who can rattle off the names of the presidents, countries and their capitols, the elements, bones and body parts. These kids can site information most of us struggle to even comprehend, yet they go on stage and repeat it like it's a game. We are three-fold like our father God. We have the physical form, the soul which basically retains our frequency, and when conditions are right, the soul will merge with the Christ or the Holy Spirit upon perfection.

To refer to Jesus as The Christ is a very accurate statement. But Jesus Christ is inaccurate. Jesus is not a title. Jesus was the physical name for Jeshua Ben Joseph, translated to English is, Jesus son of Joseph. Christ is a living entity. For want of a better explanation, the Christ is the Spirit we want to be filled with. Christ is the Son of God who manifested in full consciousness in Jesus. So you see, it is Jesus the Christ. When Jesus the Christ gave his life that made it possible for Him to become the living Spirit Son of God. That Spirit lies within each of us waiting to be awakened within our consciousness. That is how He is coming again, by being born within each of us, when we are ready. When Jesus said he will come again he meant He as The Christ, the Holy Spirit will come again. When He said He could come as a thief in the night that is exactly what was meant. He has the ability to awaken within you at any time. When He spoke of the ten virgins He was saying, you must be ready to recognize Him when He comes. If you are not prepared to recognize Him you will not know Him. You must already have your lamp filled, your consciousness filled with what you are expecting, The Christ. Then He spoke of being the Bridegroom because you will be conscious of Him and know the strength of His love personally. It will be experiential.

In discerning spirits you will find you may interpret them in different ways. One is the illusion that you are to birth the Christ. We tend to misunderstand that as a physical birth, but it is the Spiritual Birthing, as in born of the Spirit. The Christ is within you, but buried. At the Spiritual Birthing He will be brought forth and you will be conscious of the Christ within. His return is within those who seek Him. It is a sacred moment of completion. This experience will carry its own frequency. The combination of The Christ and your frequency will determine your future.

Another feeling is a sense of impending loss or ending of their life, and that is exactly what happens. You will die to what you have always been and be reborn with the Spirit alive within you. The illusion is that of an impending end. It is and isn't at the same time. In your rebirth you must understand that you are also leaving behind those you love. Not in the physical sense nor will your consciousness be obvious to them. They might notice a change in attitude or see you as more peaceful and happy than before. And you might try to explain what has happened, but they will not see or understand. They will not have 'eyes to see,' or 'ears to hear' because it is not experiential for them.

How many variations of frequencies do you suppose one entity can contain? The human body has nineteen to twenty thousand genes and lives to approximately seventy years of age. If the entity has lived many lifetimes it is safe to assume there are more frequencies than genes. There is no way of estimating or establishing a number but when evaluating the differences in people knowing that they are intricate and unique, the possibilities are endless. It is my opinion that the number of frequencies is unlimited and we can achieve any frequency, high or low, of our own choosing.

This is a great controversy for people who do not believe that reincarnations are based on frequencies established throughout our past lives. Many people teach that between lives we gather together with our group of souls to plan our next life. They believe we plan our entire healing process with these souls so they may learn compassion. Or they have murdered and now need to be murdered themselves. These are the kind of stories I have heard. I can only share what was downloaded to me, searched, and researched. The information I received was consistent. All the answers I received on planning the next life was the same each time I asked. Our rebirth is based upon our frequency. If you need to learn compassion your frequency field will draw you into the compatible life to provide those opportunities. In the human body we all live lives that are not necessarily compatible with each other, but we are with our own group of people. I am referring to our current lives and the people we interact with day-to-day. When you join a group at work or meetings, you are drawn to people you have something in common with. If someone is totally outside of your frequency you may offer a simple greeting, feel indifference, repulsion, or rejection so you move on. The same is true in rebirth. You arrive where your frequency is compatible at conception.

As I continued to research the sitting down and planning scenario, I was repeatedly informed that the only time this conversational preplanning occurred was in entities with very, very high frequencies to provide specific guidance and teachings, someone like Gandhi. Gandhi was the only reference ever used to explain this process. His purpose was to show that there is a better way than war and violence, and to teach the need to go within. Within, is where all your answers lie.

The first time I heard the scenario of sitting down and choosing this lifetime I was so repulsed that I almost got sick. How can we be so naïve to believe we would intentionally design this kind of life filled with murder, hate, war, deformities, poverty, and violence? And yet we <u>do</u> partake in these through our thoughts and choices in life. For many years I tried to come to terms with this concept, the conscious preplanning of your next life. I tried to see this type of reincarnating which was so different from what I had downloaded. But the information just kept coming back the same. It was always obvious when the information field wanted me to accept or deal with information I was given. For instance, I might wake up and the first thought I might hear is that someone I knew was not feeling well because they were very low on vitamin B 12. If I did not call and share that information with them, "they" would bug me until I did. I would repeatedly hear, behind everything I said and did, "Someone needs vitamin B 12." That would not stop until I gave them the information. These messages could come every other day, especially if I was around someone with specific health issues. Often when I consulted with a client I would wake up the next morning with information for them. I was just the receiver or the transfer of the download. The information was always accurate. Often people would become upset with me because I would call to confirm that they were improving. What I would not tell them is the senders of the information wanted <u>them</u> to become aware of their improvement and acknowledge that they were better. The recipient of the information might recognize the "not being better" part, but would not acknowledge and appreciate that they were in fact improving, not even to themselves. They always assumed I wanted to know, but it was part of the healing process, the recipient needed to "acknowledge" it in order for the healing to come to fruition. We need to be thankful and recognize when a healing takes place or it will not be permanent.

How do we plan our next incarnation? How do we take personal responsibility for our next life? How do we change from haphazard reincarnation to being a planned co-creator of our life? It is important we accurately communicate our wants and needs. When someone says they asked for something but did not get what they wanted, my first question is always, what did you ask for? I find most people are not detailed about what they want. Let's say they asked for a red dress. You have to be specific about the red dress you want. Do you want full length or short; evening or afternoon wear; zippers or buttons, fire engine red or soft red, ruffles or straight? You must provide the details to get what you want, but usually we ask for something vague and general like, I want a new car. Or, I want a new red Prius. Well, what accessories do you want? Do you want a stick shift or automatic, air conditioning, special sound equipment? You have to be specific. To begin understanding the creating process, you to have to understand the method used to communicate. Again, be specific. You must also be completely honest with yourself. Ask yourself the simple questions, such as, "Do I want what I do not have in this lifetime?" I am not referring to cars, soulmates, or material things. But things like wanting to be a dancer, pilot, ball player, inventor, or any unfulfilled dreams and desires. Do you long for someone from your past, or are you fearful of losing someone you are currently with? Really examine your thoughts and desires, because they are setting your frequency for your next incarnation, right now.

I wish I could have been born into a rich family, or I wish my parents had encouraged my talents. There are so many things buried in our psyche that can change our vibrational frequency. Like my previous story, if you are not clear about your desires, such as being with your current partner in this next life, you might become their sibling. So, if that is your desire, to be with your current spouse you must present the desire as wanting to be with them in a marriage or partner relationship, and make it clear you do not want to be in a familial relationship with them. As the creator or the one who chooses, you must be perfectly clear. We must make the choices. The co-creator part is the living energy of the universe, which will participate by helping bring together special elements to provide what you have asked for.

However, there is still more to determine what kind of life you will have. Frequencies are changed almost every second of your life. You're walking along in a good mood, content, and the entire world is good, when someone bumps into you and says, "Get out of the way." Suddenly, you are snapped out of your peaceful space into reactionary anger and surprise. If you had a frequency monitor you would see your vibrations instantly change. This happens constantly in our lives. You're exhausted, finally asleep, and the baby cries. You may love that child tremendously, but for a moment, you resent being awakened. You are not in harmony with the situation.

Life can take you out of harmony and into reaction. The most significant thing you can do in this life and the next is learning to stay in harmony and accept that 'life is perfect as it is.' Once this is accepted at your deepest level you can remain in harmony maintaining a more progressive frequency and vibration. There are many teachers and tools to help with this transition. The younger you learn the methods for this the better. There are meditation classes, yoga, gentle stretching, walking, but the key is the breath. There are numerous forms of yoga these days. So many yoga classes are taught as a good way to stretch and exercise.

When I was a yoga teacher I taught as I did in a past life, as a way for people to release and relax. The term 'yo,' means union and 'ga,' means God. So the term 'yoga,' is 'union with God.' Yoga is 'moving meditation,' which would be the same as saying, 'moving prayer.' As you go into each posture and go to your limit ask yourself, 'where am I holding,' in the body? What part of this posture is tight and restricting? Release in that area and take the posture deeper without pain. Ask yourself what is my thinking behind the holding? Is there fear, anger, sadness, hurt, loss, love, or resentment? If you feel you hate the posture and resent it then that is the posture you need to work on remembering to release the attitude. It is quite a process when you understand it. Hot yoga will bring release in the body and issues to the surface faster.

If this interests you, find a teacher who will teach you how to go deeper and when issues come up, keep reminding you that life is perfect as it is. As you think that, also ask what is the perfection here? What do I need to learn from this event? Do not get overly analytical, step back and release what you feel and allow yourself to be the observer of your reactions. I found myself caught up in a roller coaster event with a teenager that just kept escalating, because I was letting the situation run me. This was before yoga. But one day, as I was crying, worrying, and out of control, I sat back and said to myself, if this was someone else's child, I would have an answer to help them. I changed my perspective to that of detached observer and the answers came. We have to release the reactions and step back in our head to calmly observe the reality of what is happening, then readdress it or move on in peace.

As I said, there are many teachers these days, in person, on the internet, in books, and in silence you become your own teacher. I was confused for many years by the statement from Zen Master Linji, "If you meet the Buddha, kill him." However, it is really quite simple. You are your own Buddha; your own teacher is within you that is why it is said, the Kingdom of Heaven is within. That being said, it is also true that hell is within and included in our freedom of choice. In your quiet moments and moments of stress your teacher is there, do not accept any other as your ultimate teacher and bearer of truth. That is what the previous chapters are all about, finding your own inner teacher and for you the real truth. As you seek your own truth and freedom of choice within, also fulfill your desires from this life so you are not caught up living yesterday's dreams in your next life.

Chapter Eight

THE ACTUAL PROCESS

S O HERE WE ARE. WE have finally arrived at the purpose and goal of our life; to understand the path to the Kingdom of Heaven within; to attain direct communication and bliss with God. If you have skipped any part of this book, then you have skipped the process to achieve the success of being here. Your experience will mirror your commitment, and that is in completion of the process. Your entire life and all the chapters of this book have only one purpose and that is to remove obstacles in your way so you can walk upon the steep and narrow path to God. Everything about your life, your heart-felt longings, sense of wanting to go home, or the desire to feel loved have been to bring you into the physical form to become a Son of God, just like Jesus the Christ, but with greater tools and knowledge. You have come to this point to step into the Seventh Day of Creation and take your place as Perfected Man.

How does this happen? Here we must begin to erase the illusion that you are living in. To do that we need to examine the perceptions of what you have experienced, what you have lived, and what you believe to be true. Trust me; it is not as overwhelming as it sounds. In fact, it's exciting and inviting and draws you in, because your soul is calling you within. Everything you have read up until this moment has been to lay the groundwork to this process.

We have discussed lies and misperceptions that have always been a part of our lives such as 'all parents love their children.' We wish that to be true and it would be, in a perfect world. But we know it is not THE TRUTH. Our knowledge of this sad truth comes through experience, daily living, and news reports. So the real truth is, most parents love their children and want the best for them. Those parents do everything within their power to provide their children the best life they can, but some parents have been damaged or are not evolved enough to provide love and nurturing to anyone, not even themselves. The lie has been identified.

That is where we start. By recognizing or "seeing" the lies programmed into us, we start a process of sweeping them away and "seeing" only the truth, because the fact is, the truth will set you free.

STEP ONE to oneness with God is:

Matthew 7:7 ASV 'KNOCK AND THE DOOR SHALL OPEN.'

The moment you ask any question challenging your existence, or why you are here, you step one foot on the path to the process of knocking. You started the moment you realized your own parents, teachers, and preachers could not fully answer questions of who, what, why, when, and where. From the moment you began your questions and search, when you first picked up books and continued to read, you arrived at the door of your own heart and knocked on that door.

You've made the first step, you knocked. You have learned to accept and understand what you are knocking on, is your own heart. God is not outside of you, not somewhere out there, untouchable and unknowable. Man has struggled to make sense of God. Man has tried to reduce God into a human image. What man has been looking for is hiding in the last place he would look. That place is within man, that place is within you.

STEP TWO:

Matthew 7:7 ASV 'SEEK AND YE SHALL FIND.'

This is exactly where we are at this very moment. We are going to become as little children eager to learn the ways of God so we can enter into that peace. Little children are full of questions, empty of misconceptions (which I hope the previous chapters have helped remove), and eager to learn.

Again, we must return to the Bible and be the watchman at the gates whose purpose is to watch your thoughts and beliefs, prevent unwanted information from taking root as fact, and to remove misinformation. Let's return to the information on your very birth.

*John 3:5 ASV 'Jesus answered, 'Verily, verily, I say unto **thee**, except one be **born of water and the Spirit**, he cannot enter into **the** kingdom **of** God.'*

People have taken this statement and intertwined it with 'being saved.' The religious doctrine of being saved has always eluded me. You go and confess that Jesus is the Son of God. That is admitting you know the Truth and the Truth shall set you free. It will start the process of being born of the Spirit but it is not the same thing. This confession is actually a request because someone has invited you to come forward in the church stating that you know Jesus is the Son of God and now you want to learn. You want to be born of the Spirit but the religious "lie" is that you are immediately filled with the Holy Spirit and born again. No, this person has come forward stating he is ready to be filled with the Holy Spirit and commit his desire to learn how to accomplish this.

By telling this individual he has been saved and born again of the Spirit leaves this person lost and dangling in the misperception that is a lie inside of him. What he thinks he is cannot be true. This is why so many people walk away from church or return to their old ways because nothing has changed and no one was there to teach or guide them. So what is the Truth? This person must now do exactly what you are doing. Go through the process of sorting lies from the truth to set you free. You are seeking and you will find. How often do you have to perform this ritual of sorting truth from lies? This process will become part of every moment of your life; it will be as a natural instinct, not a chore. It requires you become aware of the difference in what you hear, what you speak, and what you think, and will continue until, 'you are changed in the twinkling of an eye,' just as I was. However, at first you must develop a habit or commitment to find that truth. When you make that commitment you no longer desire to hear, speak, or think anything that is not true. Your mind will be in a state of perfection and peace. For instance, I might say something like; 'it has been raining every day.' In making the statement I might hear my inner self say, 'it hasn't rained every day. It has only rained for three days and that is not the same as every day.' Even in some of our simple 'over' statements we are not telling the exact truth and through this journey, our mind begins the process of sorting out what is fact and what is not fact.

To lay the foundation for how this works we need to role play a few probability factors you could be facing. For example, let's say you never really felt loved and wanted in your family. The more you reached out to show your love to your parents or siblings you were pushed away. The lie is, 'you are not loved and wanted.' So, what is the real truth? Start with your mother or father. What time period did they live in? Was it a time when people were openly loving and affectionate or were they more withdrawn and uncomfortable being demonstrative of their feelings? Were your parents abused? Do you think they felt loved and nurtured? Were they taught how to love and nurture their own children? Were demands put on them, even as young children, such as helping provide food to feed the family? I'm sure you see this process. Go back to the source of your judgment of others and see what prompted their behavior. Within that process lays repentance. You have judged your parents for not loving you the way you wanted or needed, so now you are repenting, re-experiencing in your mind the events that brought you to this point. You are seeing the truth of why they are unable to express their love; the real truth is they have no skills to show you that you are loved, because they had no way to learn that skill.

The reality is they most likely loved you all along but the only "training" they had was to show you that love was providing a life for you. And it might also be possible you have the misfortune to be born to parents who abuse you, because they only learned abuse. It is even possible you could have been abandoned, or given up for adoption. However do not mistake 'abandoned' and 'adoption' for similar words. Most mothers or parents who give a child up for adoption suffer tremendous pain and loss making that sacrifice for the good of the child. Again, what is the reason and why was that choice made? Sometimes finding these answers can take you into methods of self-healing or professional therapy, but it is a necessary part of the process at this time. When you truly look at the 'why' of a person's behavior you start a deep healing process that begins with understanding, acceptance, and forgiveness. Out of that understanding you can develop a true and deep sense of compassion. This compassion now starts to knock at the door of your heart, where Christ or the Holy Spirit lives. As this compassion grows into a sense of love, it seeks the heart to show that love. And, one day the flood gates of your heart will open and the Christ or Holy Spirit will be born within you.

You can probably begin to see the process of how this takes place, but there are even deeper truths and lies you might need to deal with such as teachings in the Bible. For instance, homosexuality. Who came up with that term? What does it really mean? What does the Bible say and who actually said it? One issue we have not explored is the books in the Bible. In order to proceed, we must stop and look at this truth. Who decided which books would be in the Bible? If you are like me you assumed God must have been in control of that. Then I discovered God was <u>not</u> the one who chose those books. In three-hundred-and-twenty-five A.D. Constantine formed The First Council of Nicaea which was the first ecumenical council of the Church. Most significantly, it resulted in the first uniform Christian doctrine, called the Nicene Creed. As previously stated, it was this council that determined what books would be in the Bible.

You can verify this yourself if you want all the details as I did. What I found is there are twenty-two books mentioned in the Bible that are completely missing. At that time there were many writings considered a part of the Bible. Many of those spoke extensively about reincarnation and other facts that Constantine was not interested in. So it seems they had a meeting one night to decide which books to keep and which books to leave out. There was much opposition within the counsel about which books to keep and which ones to throw out. So, Constantine informed the members who agreed with his choices to come to the meeting and overlooked the ones who disagreed. Once the preferred members arrived, they locked the doors to prevent dissenters from voting. Thus you have the current books of the Bible with twenty-two missing and many more just simply gone. To learn more about the purpose and goals of Constantine the web is full of information, but remember to read 'Google Scholar' and not just generalizations and opinions.

As you can see, there are many lies and misconceptions. Hopefully you are beginning recognize facts you do not really know, the judgments you have made, and erroneous feelings you have because other people are just doing the best they can. Can you see how this has built your own illusions and misconceptions about what reality is, and who and what you are? As these lies fall away, one-by-one, it opens that door we knocked upon and we find the truth about ourselves, life, and God. As that happens we are increasing the rate of vibration of our entire being. The more you increase your rate of vibration the faster you manifest what you want and need. This brings us back to the story of the car. You might be thinking, "Hey, I am on my way to my life's desire, who cares about the car?" To which I say, "Patience, this is just to make a point." Now, theoretically you have healed the sense of unworthiness that kept cancelling the energy to manifest the car, or whatever you wanted to manifest. You are also increasing your rate of vibration which makes it possible to manifest bigger, better, and faster. So your probability of success in manifesting your goals and desires will increase, but by now manifesting becomes a lesser desire for THINGS and those wants begin to slip away. That sense of 'being called home,' is more enticing as you get closer. What once seemed to matter has been replaced by this longing for home, to return to the point of your own beginning, and to complete the process of evolving to become the human God created when He said, "It is finished."

We do not have complete information about how this transition occurs. As you erase lies and replace them with truth, you are clearing obstacles along your path. As you continue to do this the obstacles reduce in size becoming very small along the way. Eventually, they are gone. I use to see myself as walking in a high wire act. Lies fell to one side, truths fell to the other. As they no longer held me, I was free to continue the walk until, at one point not of my choosing, the wire, the lies, and the truth all fell away. There was nothing but God filling me with unconditional love until it was almost suffocating, but so glorious I didn't care.

There is a parable for our day and time that will hopefully help to explain what is going on. For the first time in the history of known human existence we actually have a small example of what communication with God resembles. The best comparison I can use to help explain this is that we are like computers. Think back to the first desktop personal computer you were aware of or have ever heard of. There were numerous ones in many shapes, sizes, and abilities. They were totally independent and very limited within their own capacity. The first one I knew of held an amazing and massive forty MB's of memory. The system programming came on a floppy disk and there was a second disk drive you used as memory. It only had the basics, similar to early man. Like man it came with few tools and few capabilities. We thought it was amazing and were anxious to own one. Some time passed before the next generation of computers came out with more memory, but the software was mostly run from five-and-one-half inch floppy disks and you had to save information to floppy disks, it was limited. We have to remember the first several generations of computers were totally stand alone and could not reach out to anything like the internet. Computers now, evolve very rapidly, changing so fast it is next to impossible to keep up with the most resent models. In comparison, humans are evolving very, very slowly.

As computers grew, they had a modem which reached out to get small amounts of data stored "somewhere." The connections were slow and unreliable, but you could find limited assistance with a variety of searches, very much like later man and his quest for sun Gods, Gods of the sky, Gods of the earth, etc. Again, the growth continued and soon a three month old computer system was out of date as new technology appeared. In that era, there were CRT's, consoles, keyboards and monitors appeared to be stand-alone, but in fact were connected through phone wires to servers that held all the information and collected data. One person would sit at each CRT and input information to the servers. These servers would collect all the data from multiple CRT's. They could be nationwide or in a small area. Suddenly, search engines started appearing out of nowhere. The first viable one was WebCrawler. Before long we had MSN, Mozilla, Google, Bing, and so on. We had search engines that hijacked your searching and lead you where <u>they</u> wanted you to go. When I say they would hijack your searching, you might be using Mozilla and go to a site and some startup site might start running like About.

com. Once you are hijacked, it can require major work, research, and cleaning to get rid of the culprit. This is a good comparison to a religion or cult that keeps you brainwashed in simple ways like making you feel guilty, to more complex ways of taking complete control. They manage to keep you locked into their way of thinking and being. But, if you work at it, you can find the way to deprogram yourself and reconnect to your ultimate search for God.

Today we have so many things attacking the integrity of the World Wide Web and our private information that we now have all kinds of firewalls, anti-virus protection, and malware trackers. And we have a negative collective energy that can, and will if you let it, take you from your path. That negative energy loves to control and mislead people, keeping them in their suffering. Just like the saying, "Misery loves company," so does the collective negative energy. It doesn't want you to know the truth and will do what it can to keep you trapped and ignorant. Add to this how technology has taken over our banking, the way we view television, our phone systems, and messaging. Computers have evolved into all aspects of our lives. And just when we thought it could not get any more confusing they gave us the Cloud. How thankful are we that our pictures and personal lives can be shared without our permission? We do not need Big Brother watching us because, EVERYONE is watching us. And you might wonder, 'Where is the Cloud?', 'What does it consist of?', 'What are its capabilities?', 'What is it up to?', and the big one, 'Is it safe?'

There are many people who teach and claim to connect with something outside of themselves. They convey a need for man to learn unconditional love, acceptance of all humanity, and compassion. Like the connection to the Cloud, these people reach out and communicate in a selective manner. They have developed skills to find the true information they seek and pass it on to the masses. A lot of computer users access and send information to the Cloud and are totally unaware of it. Conversely, certain individuals can reach out to just the right portion of an information system just outside of normal human informational systems. They reach out and obtain information that, up to now, seemed unavailable to modern man. Everyone receives information from this God, or this mass 'collective higher consciousness' every day labeling it their subconscious or intuition. Most people just ignore the information that comes to them and continue their normal routine. But information is available to everyone, every moment of the day.

If it were not for that communication or computers I would not be writing at all. I would have nothing to write and the manual process would be slow and cumbersome. All my life I have heard, "As above, so below." Our reference or terminology of God is, He is above and we are below. So here this term applies. We have computers designed so we can reach far beyond our own knowledge and capabilities, to retrieve information and maintain a more progressive style of life. And with this concept, of reaching beyond one's self, we have begun to realize that never before in history have we had such a clear example of who we are, what our purpose is, and what we are doing here. This is an exaggeration of statements because only a few people are beginning to see the basic patterns, directions, and purposes of life. But there must be a beginning and they are pathfinders who are here as teachers. As we become more aware of them, the opportunity to evolve increases.

I want to digress long enough to mention that there are many people who hate computers because it is too much trouble to learn them. The same is true with finding out who we are and what God is. For some it is too much trouble, too much self-responsibility. There are many people who have been taught that the government owes them a living, so they do not work, at least not so they get caught at it. They allow the rest of society to work and pay the taxes that provide them with money. They do not want self-responsibility. This is the story of the Garden of Eden.

If we just wanted to live in a perfect place within parameters we would still be there, but we are not all the same and most humans want to be more than complacent. God, like computers, is there for us to plug into. Just as a toaster will not toast without being plugged in, mankind cannot evolve without reaching out and plugging into God.

I have said this consistently throughout this book, we are evolving. This is our purpose. This is our goal. This is who and what we are. So, what does that mean and what are we evolving into and out of? What were we and what will we be?

A human being is a perfect, organic, self-replicating, self-sustaining, conscious, thinking, reasoning computerized system with total freedom of choice. Before you get too upset, hear me out. There are so many subtleties and intricacies to this statement. Let's begin by looking at how this works and how much like present day computers we are.

We are an organic life form. We are self-sustaining in that we feed ourselves and transport ourselves. We have a limited ability through nutrition, supplements, medicine, etc. to heal and maintain the body. We are self-replicating. We are not manufactured, we make new versions of ourselves all the time, and we are programmed. If you doubt you are programmed then we will get into the programming process. You are made up of DNA which are the programs your parents carried around. Within recent years researchers have discovered that not only your body and ability to learn is in your DNA, but also your emotional capabilities or restrictions are handed down from your parents. That means doing as your parents have done is not just a matter of observation, but doing so is motivated and patterned by your DNA.

Your parents, school teachers, leaders, news media, television, computers, and information systems provide information which you store and evaluate at a subconscious level to decide what you accept as relevant and non-relevant, true or untrue. Every person we come in contact with, whether live or recorded, affects our programming in either a negative, positive, or indifferent way. Of all this information you ingest you develop the self, the ego, the personality, and your judgment or evaluative system. You become what is known as 'you.' Are you a Mac or a PC? Are you a desktop or a laptop? Are you male or female, son or daughter, professional or blue collar worker, American, Asian, or European, dumb or smart, married or single, etc.? We have many labels attached to ourselves as identifiers. Who would we be if we did not have labels?

Would a rose by any other name be as sweet? Well, would it? If you were not Bob, Sally, Jane, or Pete would you still be the same person? It is almost as though others owned us. If you were not told you were a son, daughter, mother, father, dumb, lazy, ugly, smart, or beautiful what would you be? We are labeled in every part of our lives. Pilot, farmer, housewife, just some of the many labels we inflict upon ourselves to limit us. How many labels make our lives more complicated while too few labels can limit us? Without adequate labels we can't get a job. We can't win in the labels game, but try this. Try to erase the labels given to you and see who is left behind. Make sure you focus on the negative as well as the positive labels like failure, success, victim, perpetrator, unloved, owned, rejected, etc. Can you see that each of us is the result of moment to moment programming? Of all the things you learn, the fact that you are your own personal programmer is the easiest lesson. The main point of that lesson is to let go and be what you truly are.

It has only been within the last hundred years that medical researchers have discovered the location of the human firewall. The 'thalamus' has many duties in the body but the major job it performs is to filter the information we receive. The thalamus is the 'gatekeeper' or 'watchman at the gate' that actually regulates which information gets to the brain for processing. So there is a firewall, but firewalls are not perfect and do not only keep out hackers and unwanted interference, they can also block good information, emails, and correspondence we would like to have. If your firewall is blocking information you know you need, you begin the process of correcting the programming within that firewall to make it service you according to your needs. Those same aforementioned medical researchers are discovering ways to assist the evolutionary process to allow an increase in the information we receive from a needed source. I find that pretty exciting because we will no longer need to look outside of ourselves for teachers or guides, but be able to access that wisdom at our own discretion. It will be necessary, as with the computer, to make the decisions of what information is desirable and what isn't. That is again called the discerning of Spirits which is how we will move into the perfected man of the seventh day. That is the time when the asking of questions will diminish and fall away.

And here we will stand at STEP THREE which is:

Matthew 7:8 ASV *'FOR EVERY ONE THAT ASKETH RECEIVETH;'*

If you ask, you receive. This is where you get to ask the really hard question, "What should I ask for and what will be given unto me?" This is a long journey, but what is the purpose of all this? You will now begin the process of becoming perfected man, Son of God, Born of the Spirit, and to put that into more sensible terms, you will be the directed co-creator of who and what you are with God as the other part of the creating. You will be in partnership with God in manifesting your life choices.

Chapter Nine

NEW BEGINNINGS

NEW BEGINNINGS ARE COMING AND we must be ready. The first step in helping our fellow travelers awaken is to "accept them for who and what they are." We all require acceptance as an individual before we can start growing spiritually, without that growth we stay in the consciousness we are in right now. Lack of acceptance as a unique, one-of-a-kind individual is the single most influential problem we experience in human form. Without acknowledgement and acceptance of who and what we are makes struggle senseless in one way or another. It is the cause of dis-ease in the body and in the mind.

The process of acceptance does not require you delve into the personal life or history of anyone, but to simply accept them unconditionally. We may know they are spiritual beings however; it is not our job to inflict that information upon them, but to simply let them know we see them. We must learn to see them for who they are and honor their path as it is. We cannot inflict our judgment and interference upon their Karma or path of growth. You must say to yourself, "I see you for who and what you are and accept you for that. I know you have problems. I know you struggle. I know you want more, but I see that which is within you and accept it. As I accept it, I can support you to be all that you dream you can or want to be."

Do you realize how empowering that simple statement can be to anyone who is suffering? These are the questions we all seek answers to and now you can have those answers. What do you want? Why are you here? What are you seeking? We are here to find out who we are. Accept who we are, Children of the Unknowable (unlabelable) God. There is no name. There is no description. What we call God is only known by accepting and knowing ourselves, our true feelings, wants, and desires. What are we seeking? We seek our authentic self. It is that simple. That begins through, *acceptance without judgment.*

Can you imagine the power of someone simply accepting YOU? That is what the ancient and recent Masters do. They accept and see you. That is the power they have. Imagine, acceptance without need or desire. A Master is complete within themselves and have no need or desire from others. That is the power of awakening, unconditional acceptance. This is what our future needs to be based upon, acceptance. Can you accept a mass murderer is what they are without judgment and condemnation? Can you look deeper at the pain and confusion in their lives that brought them to this horror? Every person gets up from their bed striving to do the best they can whether that is from a deranged mind or a healthy mind. The sick do not have the ability to know their thoughts are outside of healthy thoughts. Most likely the murderer has reason to be drawn to murder from experiences and influences in their life. Sometimes that influence comes from voices only their sickness hears. The question is, can you love them without judgment? Can you help them without judgment?

The ability and opportunity to develop a strong progressive life style for the world lies within our ability to see ourselves as evolving beings who can love ourselves and the world. Once we have acquired the ability to love ourselves and others totally, the rituals and religions will fall away to be replaced by a strong mature society. The need for religious gatherings will be replaced by the need for smaller groups that can support each other in life situations. The existing buildings could be transformed into places of teaching and learning. The first lesson from conception and all through life should be to remember the lifetimes you have witnessed or lived. Why go to history class to learn what you have lived and learned in previous lifetimes? What talents did you have in your previous life experiences? Were you a musician or any type of artist? Were you a healer? Possibly your interest was in new ways of growing foods and sharing them with others. Wouldn't it be fabulous if you could go to a building filled with people who had the same interests so you could brainstorm and share your talents with each other? Imagine meeting others with your interests and having the ability, without feelings of insecurity, to openly share everything you know and learn from others. Can you imagine how much faster we would progress? These ways of living are possible for us as we evolve. We can solve world hunger; instead of government paying farmers to stop farming, we could build the farms back up to provide for the community.

That is just the beginning of what can happen at the moment the seed of the Christ awakens, but it requires developing the perception of what you are. As that germinates within the acceptance of self, the Christ is born. The moment the birthing process begins it is like the crucifixion, which is about leaving the land of the dead and being born into a Spiritual Being. Easter morning is all about rising up as the Christ within. Ok, so it's not that easy. But, acceptance followed by the perception of living as a Spiritual Being is the process of labor pains that births the Christ. This process goes on day after day. It is evolution. You are evolving into that Perfect Man.

What child would not want to go to school to focus only on their field of interest and share their ideas with others who are adept in that field already? It is possible that a being we consider a child is adept already and others would learn from this child. We have only to become the leaders to know the conception of a child is the welcoming of an ancient entity into our homes, to see what they bring in the way of talents and abilities. It would be a process, preparing the way for this new being to remember and share all they bring with them. The experience would be one of new adventure allowing a child to mature into the lifestyle they are already use to. Imagine generations of being a scientist and bringing with you all that you have learned lifetime after lifetime. How much could you possibly have to offer?

I find myself in a dream world of life sometimes. It would be a world without organized religions, schools, and world governments yet filled with sharing, cooperation, abundant food, clean water, necessities, and fun too. What would your fantasy be for the betterment of all of life, including yours? What would you do with the schools, churches, temples, government office buildings, rules and regulations? How could they be made useful contributors of day-to-day life instead of being closed down, left empty and decaying? What can you do to create that by beginning right now? What would you have to give up in order to create a utopian society without negative fall out? The world is vast. The talents are endless as are the possibilities. Today, right now with each breath, each thought, each longing and desire we have the potential to create a world that is exactly what we want. We could image-into existence all our dreams. Do not think of the what-ifs or of all the people who have no idea what we are imagining. Just take care of your own thoughts and creating.

Which office building, school, or church would make the best greenhouse to grow beautiful vegetables, and who do you know that would love to work there in the coldest winter under grow-lights and perfect conditions? Then again, what about nurseries for human babies where parents and infants are assisted in helping them remember. Most children, even now, have memories of their past lives but sometime before age seven an undefined trauma drives it out of them and they join the ranks of normal forgetfulness and the drudgery of survivalist thinking. So image-in how you could design a system that would help utilize the knowledge and talents buried within waiting for someone to unearth them. The possibilities are endless. We are limited only by the misconception that we are limited at all.

We are unlimited beings who can ascend to any heights we envision and imagine. The only thing that limits us at all is our perception of who and what we are. Don't waste one more day worrying about what hurt you as a child or even yesterday. My favorite exercise is to ask my students to take a deep breath, and blow it out, now go back and change it. That is how much power we have over the past. It is gone. It is done. Take the lesson it offers and move on to create a wonderful life. Most people will tell you this is a school. I tell you this is an incubator for the evolution and perfection of man. It is an opportunity to learn what the freedom of choice is. Right now you have the greatest freedom of choice and that is to usher man into the evolution of the perfect life that will take us beyond our perception of the Garden of Eden. There is no longer a limitation, sorrow, or pain which usually comes from unfulfilled expectations, needs, and desires. As readers you have the opportunity to be the pioneers to takes us to greatness.

I spent my entire life in rejection and fear to travel this journey that is only now just beginning. I have something to share with you before I leave. It's all about me and everyone else. I came into this world, in this lifetime as everyone else has. I forgot where I was from. I had no idea of my purpose. I was the youngest of six kids. I was blessed with friends. People who found me interesting and complicated, often misunderstood my desire to help set them free. All of these experiences and people have been more than a gift to one who has challenged life and is coming out a winner.

EMOTIONS are the engine that drives the thoughts that create or manifest your everyday life. The ultimate point of all of this writing is to help you 'see' that we are in all reality the birth Children of the King of the Universe and All Creation. He is waiting for us to return home to Him so He can give us the Keys to our inherited Kingdom. That Kingdom is this world that we can create into anything we want it to be. And it took all this time for me to know that 'amen' only meant, So Be It.

Bonus Chapter Ten

CHEMICAL SEPARATION FROM GOD AND SELF

I HAVE INCLUDED THIS CHAPTER BECAUSE, although you do not need to follow this to evolve, the world we live in today is so filled with chemical influences I felt it was important enough to mention.

When I was in my late twenties and I had the strangest realization. As I said, there wasn't much money and four children to feed. So car tires were not replaced as often as they needed. However, I noticed that if I woke up worrying I could have a flat tire, low and behold, I would have a flat. So I wondered if I was being intuitive and knowing it is going to happen. Or by fearing a flat because there is no money, causing the tire to go flat? So the next time I woke up thinking I would have a flat tire, I told myself that I do not need a flat tire. There is no reason for the tire to be flat and I reject the thought. That day passed and I did not have a flat. That is when I began to realize that we are creating events not just using intuition.

Having discovered that we are the creators of our lives I asked, what stops us from being conscious co-creators with God in our own lives? What do we not understand? How can we create consciously? There are so many elements that influence and alter our ability to consciously create the life we would like to live whether that life is a success in relationships, making a living, or serving God. There are elements that preachers, doctors, and psychologists seem unaware of or choose to ignore because they have no drug to treat it and no qualified method of testing for it. The only real test is personal journaling about how you feel and charting events that surround your pain and dis-ease.

This information is about one of the major, unrecognized stumbling blocks in our pathway to reality. M.C.S. (Multiple Chemical Sensitivities) cannot stop us from finding the God within but it can certainly make it more difficult to maintain our focus, goals and desires.

As we look at our judgments, forgiveness and searching, we need to address the effect health has on our emotions and decision making abilities as well as our ability to stay focused and meditate. Your mind makes your choices but emotions are the energy that drives or brings them into manifestation. Please remember that the foods you eat, the state of your health or your emotional turmoil will not prevent your transition. However, there are aspects of these that can make it more difficult to achieve and maintain once you do accomplish this goal.

The chemical world we live in interferes with being our better self. It is not a new problem and it began with the ability to generate fire at will. It prevents many people from being able to calm their minds and focus, much less meditate. Even though it won't prevent you from evolving, it can certainly cause delays. That delay can come from violence in the cities to the simple angry disposition of most smokers, and I don't want to hear about natural tobacco. Arsenic is natural and I am not putting it on my cereal. I am not saying every smoker is irrational, but I am saying that smoking affects mood and emotions. Poisons in the brain instead of good clear oxygen are the cause of so many mental diseases as well as anger and violence that it is almost impossible to identify and name them all. No matter how natural you claim a cigarette to be, it is still smoke and smoke decreases oxygen to the brain and body.

This condition is called Multiple Chemical Sensitivities and has many causes. Most people actually suffer from this condition to a degree. It may come from a reduced immune capability or the body's inability to process repeated toxic overload. Some people have minor reactions others debilitating symptoms. Because it is rarely discussed or acknowledged few people realize that reactions to toxic chemicals can be the cause of how they feel. For instance, every time my husband worked on his car or mowed the lawn he was angry. Without fail, after he was in gasoline exhaust fumes, you could not say anything that he would not respond by yelling for no real reason. For one thing, my husband and I never fight. But fumes from the car, heavy traffic, or mowing the lawn would set him off. We discovered that over-the-counter strength lithium would prevent a reaction, and before he started his project around fumes he would take a natural lithium supplement. It stopped the anger before it started.

That was nothing compared to his occasional outbreak of screaming senselessly, again seemingly without provocation. You would not even have to speak to him and he would become violent throwing and breaking things. It is difficult to say how often this would happen because it was almost thirty years ago but I knew I could not live with these unprovoked temper tantrums that scared me to death. These horrific outbreaks would require days of recovery for both of us. His reaction to the events left him apologetic, embarrassed, and subdued. It took me to a place in my past where violence was a normal day. Finally I noticed these outbreaks would only occur after his consumption of very rich ice cream. Yes, it was ice cream, ice cream of the richest and most delicious kind. When I talked about this he agreed the outbreaks were always after ice cream. Luckily he did not have to give it all up. We tried the ice milk and frozen yogurts. As long as they were not the richest, sweetest and cream heavy ice cream he is fine. I look back now and it is only by the grace of God that someone did not annoy him at the wrong time and get seriously injured. As I said, we do not fight except for a vicious three minutes a year when we are overly tired and stressed. But it does clear the marital air for a year and, no, we do not schedule it.

A doctor would have little ability to diagnose the cause of his outbursts because they lack professional studies and information on M.C.S. I am certain the anger would have prompted both counseling and drugs eventually and the anger would have controlled his life and our future.

On the other hand, my reactions were becoming spacey, freezing cold and the need to go into a deep, sick sleep. Often times the reaction would cause a horrible, intolerable headache and also low energy and an inability to think followed by days of deep, unjustifiable depression. Sometimes I would be overcome with sneezing and yawning which would then be followed by a spacey feeling, cold and the need to sleep. Many people have a rapid heartbeat and a feeling of shakiness inside. The symptoms are almost as numerous as the toxins that attack us every day.

So what is M.C.S. and how does it affect us? It is not a debilitating disease all of the time but many people with M.C.S. are classified as disabled due to symptoms of the condition and are never actually tested nor recognized as being victims of M.C.S. Doctors love to run tests and brush this condition off as migraine headaches, fibromyalgia, Chronic Fatigue Syndrome, Epstein Barr, Mitral Valve Prolapse, and more obscure diagnosis. The fact is most people will have these same test results no matter what you are dealing with and the doctors will dismiss you with one or more of these names and medications, for pain, depression, or insomnia. The better way of exploring this condition is to keep a calendar of your symptoms and find out for yourself what you are reacting to and avoid the food or chemical.

The list of offending chemicals is so long it would be difficult to list them all without devoting an entire book to them. It is amazing how many stories I hear of people who are acting outside their normal behavior who are most likely doing so because of exposure or overload of toxic chemicals.

These chemicals decrease oxygen to the brain, agitate the nervous system, drastically increasing free-radical damage caused by very high levels of oxidative stress which is known to cause between two-hundred and two-hundred-fifty diseases. In the last fifteen years there has appeared an Nrf2 supplement that will reverse oxidative stress by thirty to forty percent in thirty days. There are many hazardous snacks on the market and ineffective supplements that do not even come close to treating oxidative stressor anti-oxidants as they claim to be. Doctors continue misdiagnosing or ignoring M.C.S. as one disease after another. Because doctors try to alleviate the symptoms by prescribing a variety of addictive drugs we are becoming a world of drug addicts which prevents us from functioning on a conscious level at all. In fact, many live in an unknown state of chemical or drug induced stupor.

I know this personally because I lived it and continue to live it. However, I have learned to understand what is going on and compensate for it. When I was twenty-seven I was diagnosed as a paranoid schizophrenic with bi-polar episodes. So I went off the drugs/meds, stopped smoking, did a detox and it magically improved. In my seventies I am medication free but not symptom free, yet. I have volumes of saved medical records to prove what doctors have put me through. Between the ages of sixteen and thirty I was hospitalized thirty-two times. Six of these were due to childbirth and the rest was poor medical care leaving me very sick and over medicated. I look around at a world in the exact same condition only most people choose to stay on the drugs. Am I against doctors? No, but what I am against are closed-minded so called medical professionals. Some doctors today look at whole body/mind medicine and it is growing. But it is not enough and we must take responsibility for what we breathe and put in our bodies.

It has bewildered me over forty years that there never seems to be any comments about the unusual mental and emotional state of "good people" who seemingly lose control and commit murder or drive cars into a group of people and other violent events. If documented and tracked it would become obvious chemicals cause this type of reaction in people. At one point in their lives most people become so hurt and angry they want to inflict injury and harm onto another person who has hurt them. But the majority has the ability to remain rational, take a deep breath and move on. People who live in or are exposed to constant chemical poisoning do not have the self-control and ability to rise to their more rational thinking and to accept that their reactions are extreme. Because of the lack of good oxygen in the brain, chemical toxins and allergic reactions to chemicals these people lose control and someone suffers or dies at their hands. Friends and family are astonished when a loved one goes out of their mind to commit vicious, unexplainable acts.

I recently had an encounter with a man who was put in lock-up and had gone through years of therapy. Everyone thought of him as sick and inconsiderate when in fact he was just in one major chemical reaction after another. They threw heavy doses of Lithium and anti-anxiety medications down his throat and soon he was in danger of becoming a medically induced zombie. By the grace of God he is doing much better today and understands that he is healthy when away from drugs, chemicals and cigarettes.

It is not just lung cancer that kills smokers and second-hand smokers. It is also the massive amounts of oxidative stress put on their bodies and the bodies of their loved ones. But we have to take into consideration that all the carcinogens in the world are the greatest source of increasing oxidative stress in the body. Today there are very few doctors who deal with Multiple Chemical Sensitivities, but if you have unresolved mental and physical health issues you should consider it as a possible cause not just a symptom. Also consider an Nrf2 activator that is the subject of many papers and is being researched by drug companies so they can adulterate a natural herbal remedy into something artificial filled with side effects for financial gain. Nrf2 contributed to my body's ability to withstand being bombarded by all the chemicals and allergies in my world, decreased my depression and stopped the headaches in four days.

But we live in a chemically polluted world whether it is herbicides and fertilizers on the farms or diesel and exhaust fumes in the cities. There is so much discussion today about GMOs and all I can think of is the kids I use to know who had baby-sized teeth as adults because they lived next door to a turf farm that used chemicals constantly. When the wind blew, which was often, it carried chemicals all through the neighborhood contaminating air, soil, and homes. The entire family was riddled with mental and physical health issues, poor learning skills and especially heart disease. They were all on Medicaid and Medicare and saw lots of doctors who got paid to keep them under their care and sick. Slowly that family is dying off in their youth.

My entire point of going off in this direction about health and chemicals is simple. How can you think about and create a good life from this mental state? Most people create their lives from the mental and emotional awareness of havoc, lack, deprivation and illness. This is part of how we develop negatively and an example of why we have homeless people. Homeless people are on street corners in the worst of the pollution. They stand there breathing nothing but exhaust fumes. I personally cannot even walk or run on heavily traveled streets for that very reason. You observe their eating habits and you immediately notice they lack quality food and nutrition. How can a brain function properly without quality air or nutrition? Then add alcohol and drug addictions. Have you talked with many beggars? I spoke with a man who had been homeless for ten years. He seemed very intelligent but the more we spoke the more I realized he was very confused and irrational.

It is probable that if you would take a healthy individual, put them on a street corner with limited fresh water and a bad diet, you would convert that person to mentally unstable within a short period of time.

One example that comes to mind is of a very stoic, serious, and self-controlled person I knew. He cried so easily. I found it interesting because people who fly on planes a lot, as he did, or are in and around propane, natural gas, automobile, and plane exhaust fumes cry a lot and very easily. Many people think they are not in control of their emotions or, on the other extreme, are especially loving and sensitive when in fact they are having a reaction to chemicals.

Let's say you have not seen your Auntie for years and you believe that is why you go from being a stoic person into a crumbling, crybaby the moment your plane lands. Think again. It more likely is due to lack of quality air and an abundance of chemical poisoning. Then add the actions of some who do not understand the effect on others, decide to spray more chemicals like perfume and hair spray while you are inside an enclosed plane. Many people go off to very expensive detox clinics when all they really need to do is take Nux Vomica Homeopathic Remedy, which helps decrease your reaction, and simmer one cup of white vinegar in a gallon of water to detoxify chemicals in their home, like carpet glue and formaldehyde. One of the easiest detoxes for the liver is two tablespoons of fresh lemon in a cup of hot water first thing in the morning; then wait thirty minutes before putting anything else in your body. It's like washing your face first thing in the morning, except you are washing your liver. And because a toxic liver is the first cause of fatigue, it helps increase your energy.

When I see parents scream in public at their children who are crying and screaming, I want to just take the parents aside and talk to them about chemical poisonings or ask, "Isn't it time for lunch and a nap?" However, what I really notice are the heavy perfumes wafting off their body, the bags under the child's eyes as well as the amounts of sugar the kids are consuming. If parents and grandparents want to help these children have a better life they need to start by removing perfumes, colognes, ALL hair spray, aftershave, room deodorants, and laundry soap loaded with fragrances. These are filled with toxic chemicals. Instead they should use natural clothes softeners, unscented deodorants, etc. When was the last time you looked at your makeup, skin lotions, creams or anything that touches your body? If I use any products with petroleum jelly in it I have insomnia or get cold chills, and go into a deep sleep early in the evening then wake at midnight for four to five hours. Most insomnia is due to chemical poisoning during the day. Petroleum jelly is the same petroleum they use to run automobiles. So get real about what is altering your life. On laundry day I would not be able to sleep for two to three nights. Then, about the time the fragrance wore off from the soap and softener and I could sleep again, it was time to do laundry and load the bed cloths with chemicals again. Luckily there are now products you can use everywhere that do not use toxic chemicals.

This subject alone requires a book of its own so let's just take a few moments to consider these young children growing up in chemically toxic homes with parents who smoke outside. They believe that will keep their children safe yet they still reek of cigarettes, perfume, hair spray, and aftershave. The residue is as toxic as direct exposure. And it's not just parents; these kids have teachers who reek of toxic chemicals. Then the schools think giving these kids white flour and sugar two times a day is nutritious. All this accomplishes is to hype them up and then two hours later they're in a stupor or asleep at their desk. In an attempt to control the symptoms of M.C.S. doctors mistakenly put them on drugs for ADD and ADHD or bipolar episodes. Some children become angry and combative not knowing what is really bothering them. Another donut and sugar juice for breakfast should make them happy, right? There are too many books on diet, the brain, obesity, etc., for me to stop and detail the effects of all of that. However, the point being, it is difficult in this state of mind to help you or your children experience calm or rationality let alone pursue a Spiritual practice.

But consider you are trying to be a conscious creator and M.C.S. is your issue; or is there a family member struggling with the symptoms and you are judging and condemning them. Maybe you should take a second look and reach out to help them. In doing so you will help yourself by becoming more compassionate of a problem you might have been totally unaware of. In turn, you can help them have quality of life.

Oddly enough these chemicals can make you manic and high functioning but unrealistic, followed by a crash into anger, anxiety, depression, ADD, ADHD, OCD, etc. What would you create from this level of consciousness?

It is obvious now that our chemical world is a big hindrance in making directed conscious decisions. What occurs next is emotional damage inflicted on children raised by chemically and emotionally damaged people. Chances are these same children have genetically inherited the same undiagnosed and untreated condition that their parents are unaware of.

What is needed is healing and the need to forgive and have compassion for others as well as yourself. Consider your parents and their toxic world. Were you damaged simply because they were chemically toxic? And what damage did their parents and grandparents, etc. create for you? Few people raised in the twentieth century were not around open fires, leaking gas appliances, and cigarette smoking. Many families grew up with wood burning stoves, propane, and fireplaces. Then look at prescribed medication, drugs, health issues, and their history of physical and mental abuse whether at home or school.

There is only one effective method to deal with this issue at this time. It is to become aware of how you are feeling physically, mentally and emotionally. I started by making notes on a calendar. My first conscious thought was waking up in the morning and thinking nobody loved me. I literally wanted to kill myself. It was horrible. I believed my life was worthless and no one would care if I lived or died. I sensed something was not right other than the fact that I was out of my head. So, I took notes on the calendar including where I had been and what I had eaten. With four kids at home it was not unusual for us to make homemade pizza on the weekend. Strangely enough, I would have this suicidal depression the morning after we had eaten pizza. The kind of depression that told me no one loved me and no one would care if I was dead. I gave up pizza and those severe episodes passed.

But that was just a tip of the iceberg. I had a friend who liked to take me to this wonderful Mexican restaurant. I always ordered a beautiful tray of nachos. I would usually eat half and take half with me. In the fifteen minutes it took to return to my office I would start yawning and sneezing. Once there, I'd yawn twenty to thirty times in fifteen minutes, so wide my jaws would hurt. This would be followed by twenty minutes of non-stop sneezing and then I would pass out, falling into a very deep sleep at my desk for about ten minutes. There was nothing I could do to prevent falling asleep. Fortunately, my boss was rarely there and people did not come into the office very often. After a nice deep sleep I'd be fine. But this happened every time so I gave up the nacho trays and narrowed my reaction down to a particular cheese they used. This becomes obvious when you make notes about what is going on in your life and around you.

The hardest one to determine was the deep depression and frequent crying that seemed to come about without any obvious source especially not the same food. I would have a horrible headache for two or three days. Then I would start crying for what seemed like no reason. I'd get upset because I was out of potatoes or the sky was blue. It did not matter. Everything set me off sobbing from a deep place in my soul. Then I realized, I live in Nevada, and every time we went to a casino I would get headaches for two days followed by one to three days of senseless crying. After the crying I would have a sinus headache from the burning in my sinus but after all that I would feel normal until the next reaction. I concluded that the crying was my brain's way of detoxing itself of all the cigarette smoke I had unknowingly exposed myself to.

Not long after my experiences at the Mexican Restaurant I had the opportunity to meet a very caring resident at the local Indian Clinic. He listened intently to my tale of woe and, much to my surprise, told me he was pretty sure he knew what was wrong with me. He asked that I return at eight o'clock the next morning for a six hour glucose tolerance test. The results showed I had reactive hypoglycemia. This meant each time I was exposed to an allergen my body would immediately burn all of its sugar leaving me with very low blood sugar which made me weak and exhausted prompting a severe headache for several hours and sometimes days. By the time I received this diagnosis I had been experiencing these symptoms for well over twenty years.

In my early forties I went to an allergy clinic for very thorough allergies tests. My arms and back became one solid wound from doing this week after week. They saw no reaction to any allergens. However, within months they realized I had something called Delayed Reaction Syndrome, which explained why there was no inflammation the next day. The redness and swelling would not occur until twenty-four to thirty-six hours later. This is why when tracking your symptoms and activities on a calendar you need to back track for at least two days to help isolate the cause. Then you need to verify the length of time it takes for your symptoms to occur to understand what is causing them. Once they isolated my response time was between twenty-four to thirty-six hours they started the testing all over again. I was given injections to take home for my husband to give me three times a day. This was back in the nineties, I've heard rumors there are a few people getting successful treatment for this condition, but I wasn't one. I was given three injections a day for one year. On that first year anniversary I asked my husband if he had seen any changes other than my transformation into a human pin cushion. He confirmed what I was feeling, nothing had improved and I quit. I became more cautious and more successful at treating myself by becoming a microscopist, studying micro-biology and reading articles on the National Institute of Health website, pubmed.gov.

My symptoms were pretty consistent from becoming hyper and very talkative to depression, headaches, anger, reactive and then withdrawn and defeated. This would be followed by one to four days of physical exhaustion. As I said previously, some of the reactions would consist of getting very icy cold followed by a need to pass out. When I would lay down and cover up I would go into a deep, sick type sleep for one to two hours. My husband is such a jewel that he would heat a quilt in the dryer and wrap me up in it to get me warm. When I would wake up I would immediately remove the covers and the reaction would be over.

Another chemical reaction I experienced was the need to sleep. I would force myself to wait till bedtime, but once I got into bed I'd go into a deep sleep then wake up around midnight and not be able to go back to sleep until the sun was coming up. I know many people reading this are saying, "I do that all the time." Change to organic soaps and softeners and examine what chemicals you have been in or are surrounded by. I do not use Glade fresheners and it is best to use no air fresheners at all. My immediate response to these chemicals is a spacy feeling, the inability to think or determine distances such as when parking a car. It is like having tunnel vision or having had too much to drink. I can focus but it takes concentration to function.

These processes would last from three days, up to two weeks depending on the severity. Although there were others who seemed to be experiencing similar problems, mine were magnified. At twenty-two I was actually diagnosed as a 'canary person'. Canaries were taken into the coal mines to determine the air quality. If the canary died, the air was not breathable. As I live and breathe as a verified 'canary person' I can tell you that the air is not healthy, nor are most foods and water.

We must remember the point to all this is that chemicals are affecting our abilities to focus, reason, stay on task, meditate, study, remember and stick to our objectives. I am still amazed that throughout this entire journey I have been able to keep focus on reestablishing communication with the God/Self and understand how to do that. But the mental, physical, and emotional turmoil has made my endeavors and goals difficult. Then add my obsession of writing it into a book to share with anyone who might be interested. It has taken me until now to address that issue.

The question you should ask yourself now is, "Are chemicals behind my inability to focus, meditate, release stress and worry or relax?" Also, "do I desire awakening enough to do what it takes to make myself stronger and healthier?" But more than anything ask yourself this question, "If my body is the vehicle for my Spirit to experience human life on this planet do I care for it as well as I do my automobile? Would I consider putting things into the gas tank, oil tank, radiator, or windshield fluid not recommended for my vehicle?" Probably not, it would be damaging and expensive. Do you take precise care of the vehicle the Spirit travels in? We know the reality of that answer. Even though awakening is not dependent upon being healthy mentally, physically, and emotionally, how can you expect to focus on your goal or be the person you want to be when you are bombarded by poisons every day? This is just another level to look at to achieve the goal we struggle against to attain this goal not only in this lifetime, but in many lifetimes.

How do we achieve the evolution of the body to contain the fully active Holy Spirit when it seems impossible to avoid these reactions? There are more questions than answers, but there are clues to the reasons you cannot focus on doing the work and staying in harmony and balance. Accept that you can be perfect one day and then, just by going to the grocery store, start a reaction all over again. Accept what is. Do the best you can. Avoid exposure and contamination as often as possible. Strengthen your body, build your immune system and understand what your distractors are. More than anything do not feel guilty and blame yourself. Just continue your path as best you possibly can. Blessings on your journey and see you on the other side.

Appendix

List of therapies and treatments that have helped me survive physical challenges.

1) If not for *Nrf2, I* would not be alive today. It is five herbs that reduce oxidative stress by thirty percent in thirty days. It is also the best in nutrigenomics research and development. At sixty-eight I was so limited I was ready to leave my body, but Nrf2 gave me my life back. For more information email intune2u2@yahoo.com

2) *Dr. Jeffrey Thompson* is the ultimate in frequency adjustment with his ground breaking work in sound therapy. He has recently had significant success in dealing with ADD, ADHD, Alzheimer and Dementia. He is by far the best diagnostician I know of and his therapies are non-invasive. For more information on what he does go to https://scientificsounds.com/ and for a consultation call *The Center for Neurological Research, Healing the Body, Heart, Mind and Spirit with Sound, 1920 Palomar Point Way, Carlsbad CA 92008-7262 - Tel: (760) 931-5333.* Email: cnr@neuroacoustic.com

3) *Hylands nux vomica homeopathic remedy* has assisted in keeping me balanced in the most severe of Chemical reactions. It literally helps everything.

4) *Dr. Antonio Calzada*, son of Dr. Jose Calzada, Tijuana Mexico – *Tel: (619) 754-4885* Email: calzadaclinic@

hotmail.com for absolutely any chronic condition where you are seeking natural healing therapies. I have literally seen miracles in the clinic.

5) *Eastern Yoga* and *Phoenix Rising Yoga* therapy have helped me with coming to terms with loving myself. You must make sure that it is true yoga and not adulterated yoga.

6) Learn the *'fire breath'* at home on https://www.youtube.com/watch?v=SQS4Ad-16v

7) The God Helmet and the author Todd Murphy explained my experience. *https://www.facebook.com/public/Todd-Murphy*

8) *Dr. Dale E Bredesen author of The End of Alzheimer's*

About the Author

Co-author of two books:

WE LAUGHED, WE CRIED; AND ALONG THE GAARTX TRAIL. Taught classes on Becoming the Best You can be where attendees changed to the careers of their dreams. I had gone from a young mother with a tenth grade education to CFO of the Kansas Planned Parenthood then on to Yoga Teacher and a consultant in Alternative Health Care. My life long dream has to be write books filled with fifty years of research to help people become all they can be. That research has taken me through multiple world religious experiences that have opened my eyes from the limited views of a country girl raised within a Christian Church to a greater under-standing of God. I now live in Las Vegas NV with my wonderful husband writing my books.

Printed in the United States
By Bookmasters